THE MYTH-MAKER

JOHN WOOD
1704–1754

by

Kirsten Elliott

AKEMAN PRESS

Published by AKEMAN PRESS
www.akemanpress.com

Photographs by Kirsten Elliott and Andrew Swift

Illustrations from *The Origin of Building*, *Choir Gaure,* and the first edition of the *Description of Bath* by permission of Bath Central Library.

ISBN 0 9546138 2 1

Designed by Niall Allsop in Bath
Printed by SRP in Exeter

Set in Frutiger, Perpetua and Sabon

ACKNOWLEDGEMENTS

I have had considerable help and encouragement from several people while writing this book. First and foremost I would like to thank Dr. Andrew Swift. He had the idea for the guided walk "John Wood – Myth-maker" which inspired this book and then persuaded me to write down my discoveries and ideas. The staff at Bath Central Library, especially the local studies librarians, have been very helpful in finding the material I needed, while Colin Johnston and Lucy Powell at the Bath Record Office have, as ever, combined efficiency with friendly service.

I would also like to thank Amy Frost at The Building of Bath Museum, and Diane Clements, Director at the Library and Museum of Freemasonry at the United Grand Lodge in London, for providing not just facts but also thought-provoking ideas and suggestions which led me into other lines of research. Members of the Bath Freemasons provided me with useful information, especially Dennis Mosley, who first alerted me to the fact that there was no record of John Wood having been a Mason.

John Wroughton, former headmaster of King Edward's School at Bath, kindly listened to my theories about John Wood's education and provided me with further information about schooling in Bath in the first half of the eighteenth century. Robin Darwall-Smith, Archivist at University College, Oxford, provided me with considerable information about John Wood the Younger's career at Oxford.

Finally I would like to thank Martin Wood, post-graduate student at the University of Bristol, for walking round the Circus with me, looking at the carved metopes. Thanks to his knowledge of symbolism in various religions, especially those current in the United Kingdom in Wood's day, he was able to suggest explanations for some of the carvings which would not have occurred to me, and a possible solution to the meaning of the Circus.

Note on spelling, punctuation, and dates

In the eighteenth century, nouns were given capital letters, as they still are in German today. I have dispensed with this in quotations, and I have also modernised spelling, except for quotes earlier than 1700, where I felt altering the spelling would take something from the writing.

Until Britain changed to the Gregorian calendar in 1752, the first three months fell into the preceding and the new year; i.e. February 1732 was called February 1731/2. I have reverted to modern usage throughout.

And if what Cicero says, when he tells us that the Druids were the Inventors of Mythology, be true; and if it be true also that Abaris wrote a Book of Theogony; we may, to the same Works, bring the whole Pagan World to be trained up in the Knowledge of Sacred Things.

John Wood: An Essay towards a Description of Bath, 1749

PREFACE

John Wood intended his book *The Origin of Building* to begin with a provocative statement. All previous accounts were imperfect, he wrote, and thus it was necessary for him to put matters right. When the printed version came out the statement was omitted. He appears to have realised that it would have offended certain influential people, although a very similar remark appears in his book about Stonehenge. I make no such bold statement: my aim is simply to add to the John Wood debate. We know so little about Wood, and the more one learns about him, the more elusive he becomes. Try to put your finger on him and he slips from under it, like quicksilver. There is so much contradictory evidence, so many gaps, that would-be biographers have often had to fill in the gaps with theories. I do not attempt to contradict those theories, merely offer alternatives.

Until 2002, the life of John Wood had not really captured my imagination. I had taken only the required amount of interest necessary for a guide and author of local books. I was more interested in people's everyday lives than architecture. However, I found his *Description of Bath* very useful, with its vivid descriptions of the city in the early eighteenth century. The exception was the first half, with its convoluted and unlikely view of history. It was while writing a new book about Bath that I decided to study Wood more closely. The man who had often seemed irritable and difficult became rather endearing. I felt sympathy for his frustration with the city's complacency, parochialism and lack of vision, something it still suffers from today. I also began to doubt about his so-called fervent belief in Freemasonry.

In 2003, a letter to the local paper from a resident of the Circus asked what events would celebrate the tercentenary of the birth of Bath's most famous architect in 2004. No reply came. It seemed that the Building of Bath Museum, which was preparing an exhibition for later in 2004, was the only official body that was working on a celebration. Even a proposed architectural festival had fallen through. So fellow-guide Terry Mitchell and I decided to run a series of tribute walks in the Bath International Music Festival 2004, not just about Wood, but about architecture in general. I suggested a short but intensive walk around the Circus, looking at the carvings. This walk, or rather the research it inspired, was later to prove crucial to my thoughts about the Circus. But first came the Bath Literature Festival. It was then that Dr. Andrew Swift suggested "John Wood – Myth-maker". His idea was that I should explain the myths that had motivated Wood not only as architect but also as author.

In the end the walk showed that he not only wrote myths – he inspired them.

One myth is that Wood was indulging in what one recent author has called "wild fantasies". Wild they may seem now, but they were not wild at the time. Part I of this book is an explanation of the various philosophies current in Wood's day, and a background to his particular interests, namely – King Bladud, Druids, and the stone circles at Stonehenge and Stanton Drew. Part II recreates the original walk, augmented with additional material. It is intended as a "virtual" walk, to be imagined from the comfort of your armchair rather than actually carried out, book in hand. At the end, I draw no definite conclusion – my aim is to simply to throw open other doors for research, which may perhaps, one day, explain the secrets and mysteries of John Wood's Bath.

CONTENTS

PART ONE
SETTING THE SCENE

1 INTRODUCTION – MAGIC, MYTHS & THE MEANING OF LIFE

In the age of the Internet, mobile phones, organ transplants and satellites in deepest space, you may think that magic holds no interest for us. However, put the word MAGIC into a search engine on the aforementioned high-tech Internet and over twenty-nine million references pop up. Put in NEW AGE and over fourteen million results are at your disposal, while even something as esoteric as ALCHEMY brings up a cool one and a half million references. Clearly, despite our apparent understanding of the world about us, we are still attracted to the arcane. Imagine how plausible, how reasonable it must have been when science was in its infancy. Except that, of course, we simply cannot imagine it. However New Age we may profess to be, even those of us who choose to shun the modern world, we cannot remove our knowledge from our brains. Technophobes who declare that e-mails and DVDs are black magic do not really believe it. They are just seeking another way to say that they find the technology baffling. Yet in the seventeenth century, great scientists such as Isaac Newton and Robert Boyle were also alchemists, searching for the philosopher's stone. William Stukeley, antiquarian and archaeologist, styled himself as Arch-Druid, and many of his archaeological theories have distinct alchemical references. What they were interested in was magic, but they saw themselves as Magi, rather than magicians. They were certainly not pagan, although theology was very much on their minds.

One man fascinated by all things arcane was Elias Ashmole. Scholar and antiquarian, born in 1617 in Lichfield, he seems to have been enthralled by any theory then current. Sometimes cited as one of the first Freemasons, he was also an alchemist, astrologer, Rosicrucian and Hermeticist, besides being interested in the Knights Templar. Yet he was no daydreamer – in fact he was extremely shrewd. His second marriage was for money, and ended in separation, although his unfortunate wife was unable to get a divorce. Instead, Ashmole kept the cash. Scientifically he had an enquiring mind, and was one of the founder members of the Royal Society. From having been born the son of a saddler, he died in 1692, the favourite of the Stuart kings, and a doctor of Oxford University. Astrology gradually took over from alchemy as his principal interest, but as late as 1672 he acquired books by Dr John Dee, Elizabeth I's astrologer, and another alchemist. It was alchemy that turned Ashmole's attention briefly to Bath when he described a tincture discovered by the last Prior of Bath, William Gibbs (also known as Prior Holloway.)

Shortly after the dissolucon of Bath Abbey, upon the pulling downe some of the Walls, there was a Glasse fond in a Wall full of Red Tincture, which being flung away to a dunghill, forthwith it coloured it, exceeding red. This dunghill (or Rubish) was after fetched away by Boate by Bathwicke men, and layd in Bathwicke field, and in the places where it was spread, for a long tyme after, the Corne grew wonderfully ranke, thick and high: insomuch as it was there look'd upon as a wonder. This Belcher and Foster (2 Shoomakers of Bath, who dyed about 20 yeares since) can very well remember; as also one called Old Anthony, a Butcher who dyed about 12 yeares since.

This Relacon I recd: from Mr. Rich: Wakeman Towne Clearke of Bath; (who hath often heerd the said Old Anthony tell this story) in Michaelmas Tearme 1651.

The last prior of Bath Abbey was yet another alchemist. Red was seen as the most desirable form of tincture, capable of performing miraculous cures, transmuting of metals and many other wonders. This belief in apparently bizarre theories was not as strange as it now appears. Indeed, as the plethora of New Age websites and the volumes of books on arcane and mysterious subjects proves, even in our sophisticated world many people are reverting to the old ideas. They are not alone. Nuclear scientists are arguing over the possibility of transmutation, although not usually from lead into gold. There is, however, a story that in 1972 the lead shielding of a Russian experimental nuclear reactor was found to have turned to gold. It should be added that this is almost certainly a modern myth!

While scientists of the seventeenth and eighteenth centuries argued about the philosopher's stone and the existence of God, antiquarians (and as we have seen with Ashmole, there was no clear distinction between the two) were trying to assimilate myths into history. One problem facing historians and would-be archaeologists was that ideas about the age of the planet were hopelessly wrong. In 1650, Archbishop Ussher declared that the earth had been formed on Saturday 23rd October, 4004 BC. This meant that what we now know were 4.5 thousand million years, a mere two million years of which relate to human history, were crammed into about six thousand years. It would not fit. Mythical tales involving everyone from Adam and Eve to King Arthur and Merlin were an attempt to explain away some of the anomalies that kept cropping up. Hard evidence such as fossils confused the issue still further. John Aubrey could only assume that they showed that the whole earth had once been covered by sea, and that the land was formed by violent earthquakes. Could this be made to fit with the history of the world as told in the Old Testament? Enquiring minds such as his were constantly coming in conflict with perceived notions based on the Bible. Great minds such as Isaac Newton's struggled to fit the Fall of Troy or the founding of Rome into a Biblical time frame. When John Wood died in 1754, the theory of evolution was still a hundred years away, but hypotheses about the age of the earth were already challenging the views of the Creationists.

Chief among the myths which proved irresistible to antiquarians was the legend of the Druids. Druids had, of course, existed – Julius Caesar wrote about them and the Emperor Claudius abolished them. But the ideas held about them by people like

Aubrey and Stukeley were incorrect, ignorant as they were of the Neolithic, Bronze and Iron Ages. They were not alone. As late as 1818, the great Tom Paine, author of *The Rights of Man*, was endeavouring to prove that Freemasonry was based on the secret religion of the Druids. At about the same time, William Danby, of Swinton in Yorkshire, was building his very own Druid Temple. John Wood was influenced by the Irish philosopher and pantheist John Toland, who set up an order of Druids in 1717, the same year that the London Freemasons set up the Grand Lodge of England. The ideas of all these people were not so different from Wood's, yet no one describes them as wild fantasies, as they do with Wood's. Indeed Stukeley is revered as a kind of father figure to English archaeology, even though, as John Wood was to point out, his ideas about Stonehenge were extremely fanciful, and his measurements, far from being the "excellent fieldwork" described on some websites, were simply wrong, adjusted to fit his own theories.

Why were so many of these strange ideas prevalent in the Age of Reason? Almost certainly because that is exactly what their proponents were trying to establish – a reason for everything they saw about them. They were hunting for the meaning of life, but without the knowledge available today to even the least scientific of minds, so much proved to be baffling. No wonder they were prepared to consider myths, magic and esoteric religions. In some ways, they were, perhaps, more open-minded than we are today, prepared to explore strange intellectual territories, risking ridicule and condemnation in doing so. John Wood's peculiar tales of Bladud, Camalodunum, and mysterious temples on Mons Badonca (Lansdown) must be seen in this context, not regarded in isolation as bizarre ramblings. What sets Wood apart is that he takes the perceived history of the Druids and develops it, placing at its centre the legendary figure of Bladud. Did he really believe the stories that he narrates in his books, or was it an attempt to give Bath a spurious pedigree to encourage culture-seeking tourists to the city? Was it borne out of a genuine pride in his home town, or was it the attempt of an outsider to win the respect of the natives? We may never know the answer, but there does seem to be evidence that he came to identify with the mythical British king. For John Wood, the magic and the myths surrounding this Celtic superman came together to provide, if not the meaning of life, then the inspiration for and driving force behind his unique works of architecture.

2 SECRETS & MYSTERIES

A glossary of 17th & 18th century arcane theories and some of the people who developed them

Many of the societies formed in the eighteenth century still survive, most notably Freemasonry. Today, its members are interested in trying to establish their true history, and distance themselves from some of the stranger societies which might, or might not, have originally influenced them. However, to understand what may have motivated John Wood, we need to know what was believed in his day. The same applies to religion. Some religious theories have become formalised, such as Unitarianism. At the time, there was a great debate between those who believed in the Trinity and those who only believed in One God, and to add spice to the mixture, there were those, like John Toland, who were pantheists. This short glossary of the secret mysteries, philosophies and the men behind them aims to explain some of the ideas which may have contributed to John Wood's writing and architecture.

ALCHEMY

Alchemy is the basis of modern science, but it is a philosophy as well as a science. Modern science has split into a myriad of specialist subjects, but alchemy takes a holistic view. Mainly associated in modern minds with the search for the philosopher's stone which would turn lead into gold, it was actually based on a search for a cure for all ills. Central to its beliefs was a study of the sun, moon and stars, and thus astrology was also important to the alchemists. Observation of the natural world developed into chemistry, physics and astronomy. Isaac Newton's researches into light were almost certainly inspired by his alchemical beliefs.

Associated with alchemy were many books of emblems, in which a series of pictures were accompanied by appropriate text. The craze for emblems began in 1531 with Andrea Alciato's *Emblematum liber*, but an alchemical collection called *Atalanta fugiens*, by Michael Maier, was published in 1617. Many other books of emblems were published, some purportedly Christian, although the pictures are often somewhat less pious than the accompanying words. The books frequently borrowed from one another, and alchemical references abound in all of them. Many of these picture books were published until well into the eighteenth century. John

Wood appears to have had access to a library of them, for emblems from several books appear on the Circus.

ASHMOLE, ELIAS 1617 – 1692

Ashmole is best known as the man who gave his collection of curiosities to Oxford University, which was the genesis of the Ashmolean Museum. Many of the items had belonged to the botanist John Tradescant, whose collection Ashmole helped to catalogue, and which he later acquired through rather dubious means. It was not only the natural world which fascinated Ashmole. He investigated and wrote upon almost every philosophy he encountered. He was friends with the astrologer William Lilly whom he met in 1646, and astrology was a lifelong interest. Another subject which attracted him was alchemy, and he purchased the library of the alchemist John Dee, Elizabeth I's astrologer, later publishing his works. In 1646 he became what was known as a Speculative Freemason, and was initiated into a lodge in Warrington. It has been said that he collected material for a History of Freemasonry although no evidence of this has been found. He wrote a book on Hermeticism and was said to have been a Rosicrucian. He was certainly interested in its beliefs and was a member of a society based on Rosicrucian ideals. This was the Invisible College, a gathering of men of science, arts and literature, who later went on to found the Royal Society.

DRUIDS

It was John Aubrey, the Wiltshire antiquarian, who accidentally started the Druid revival. In 1648, while out hunting, he came across the great stone circle at Avebury, and was inspired to make a study of it. In his unpublished work, *Monumenta Britannica*, which consists largely of his field notes, he put forward the idea that circles such as Avebury and Stonehenge were the result of a Druid culture. This idea appealed to the antiquarian William Stukeley. In 1717, as he was beginning his explorations at Stonehenge and Avebury, the Irish philosopher John Toland formed a neo-Druid group called The Druid Circle of the Universal Bond (An Druidh Uileach Braithreachas). However, Toland's interest in the Druids was rather ambivalent, for he used them to satirise the established church, thus irritating Stukeley, who, after Toland's death, declared himself to be the Arch-Druid. The Ancient Order of Druids was formed in 1781 and the Welsh Gorsedd, also inspired by Stonehenge, was created in 1792. There are still those who consider themselves to be druids.

The Ancient Order of Druids was not based on actual druidism, which involved prophesy, divination and – according to Julius Caesar – human sacrifice, but a philanthropic brotherhood. Religion and politics were excluded, but, like Freemasonry, it was a secret society. Toland had intended it to be a circle for freethinkers, and a return to what he perceived as Celtic worship of a world at one with itself. Modern druids continue this approach. They are also concerned with the bardic tradition and ecology. Some people, notably Tom Paine, in 1818, have declared that Druidism and Freemasonry are linked, and it is certain that in the eighteenth century, many people, such as Stukeley and Toland, were members of both orders.

EMBLEMATIC BOOKS
See under Alchemy

FREEMASONRY
The first definite reference to a Masonic lodge in England comes in 1641 when Sir Robert Moray, soldier, philosopher and loyal Jacobite, was initiated into a lodge in Newcastle. However, this was a Scottish lodge, the Lodge of Edinburgh, and the members were part of the Covenanters' army occupying the North of England. Freemasonry in Scotland dates back to 1599, and has been linked with the Knights Templar. Perhaps because of its proximity to Scotland, the North of England was in the forefront of English Freemasonry. Elias Ashmole was initiated into a lodge in Warrington in 1646. These lodges, which were reputedly dining clubs, but may have been secret societies for discussing controversial matters such as the return of the Jacobite kings, were based loosely on the lodges formed by stonemasons, known as operative masons. People such as Ashmole, who had no craft background, were known as speculative masons.

In 1717, a group of four London lodges met together and declared themselves to be the Grand Lodge of England. It was some considerable time before all lodges in England allied themselves to the Grand Lodge, however. York in particular had resented this interference and declared its own Grand Lodge of All England in 1724.

Freemasonry includes in its rituals a great many of the ideas which were prevalent at the time, such as Rosicrucianism and Druidism. Much of this came from a desire to be inclusive in their religious philosophy. Thus God is known by names such as the Great Architect, and, as with the Druids, religious discussion is not allowed. Freemasonry is strictly non-sectarian, and as early as 1732, the Cheapside lodge of London had a Jewish master, Daniel Delvalle. In 1723, Dr James Anderson, a Scottish Presbyterian minister living and working in London, published the *Constitutions of Freemasonry*. They remain controversial even today, although the reasons for this have changed. It is in this book that an attempt is made to trace Freemasonry right back to Adam and Eve, but in particular to link it to Solomon's Temple.

Today the United Grand Lodge of England succinctly describes modern Freemasonry as follows:

> Freemasonry is a society of men concerned with moral and spiritual values. Its members are taught its precepts by a series of ritual dramas, which follow ancient forms, and use stonemasons' customs and tools as allegorical guides.

HERMETICISM
Hermeticism is named after the Greek god Hermes Trismegistus. It is a philospohy which states that humanity is striving to be in a state of oneness with the Divine. It draws its beliefs from many Western esoteric traditions and holds that the Universe is ultimately divine. It was the translation in 1400 of what were believed to be ancient texts which brought it to the attention of Renaissance thinkers. Alchemy, numerology and cryptography were all facets of it. Despite later evidence that the texts, which

included the so-called "Emerald Tablet", were much later than first thought, it was an inspiration to such thinkers as Copernicus and Sir Isaac Newton.

JONES, INIGO

Inigo Jones (1573 – 1652) was the father of English Palladian architecture. He visited Italy on two occasions, and learnt about the works of the sixteenth century architect Andrea Palladio, meeting such Italian masters as Scamozzi. Bringing these ideas back to England, and then promoting them, he was to change the face of English architecture for ever. Sadly, his life ended in disappointment, with the outbreak of Civil War and the formation of the Commonwealth. Because he had worked as Surveyor for Charles I, he lost his job, and had his property sequestered for a time, although it was later returned. He is best known for the Banqueting Hall at Whitehall and the Queen's House at Greenwich.

Inigo Jones was fascinated by Stonehenge, but refused to believe that it was constructed by the Druids, deciding it was a Roman temple. Despite this divergence of views (Wood firmly believing in the Druidic origins of Stonehenge) he seems to have been one of John Wood's heroes. It was William Stukeley's criticism of Jones's ideas about Stonehenge that provoked Wood to conduct his own survey.

KNIGHTS TEMPLAR

The original Knights Templar date from just after the fall of Jerusalem to the Crusaders, who then needed to defend the city. A group of French knights banded together to form an order of poor knights who were linked to the Cistercians. The order became very popular, both with those wishing to join, and to those who saw them as a great defending force. Gradually, over the years, they became immensely powerful, owning property in many parts of Europe. They began to be viewed with suspicion, notably by King Philip the Fair of France. They also found themselves in conflict with the Knights Hospitallers. In 1307, Philip bullied the weak pope Clement V into letting him arrest the Templars, on the grounds that they were heretics. In most countries they were declared innocent of heresy, but in France they were persecuted. Under torture, many "confessed", including Jacques de Molay, the grand master of the order. At his trial in 1314, he unexpectedly and bravely withdrew his confession. The result was that he was burnt at the stake with his companion Geoffroi de Charnay.

The story did not end there. Legends about them grew as the order dispersed. In parts of Europe not under French control, the Knights Templar sometimes changed their name, as they did in Portugal, or joined other orders. The relevance to eighteenth-century thought is the connection, or perceived connection, between the Knights Templar and the Freemasons. It was long believed that the Knights Templar in England and Ireland fled to Scotland, and that Scottish Freemasonry adopted the rituals of the banned order. The Jacobite Chevalier Ramsay, exiled in France, is thought to have made an oration to the French Freemasons in 1737, in which he declared the Knights Templar to have been the founders of Freemasonry. A variation on this belief was that the stonemasons who had worked for the Knights Templar were the founders of the early lodges. Whether this is true or not is irrelevant. Freemasons – and their opponents – believed it in the seventeenth and eighteenth centuries. There may have been some truth in it. The order had owned property in Scotland and Yorkshire.

It was also believed that the Knights Templar were interested in the hermetic tradition, and had brought alchemy from the east to Europe. Perhaps due to their secrecy and their wealth, rumours about them flourished. There were stories that they worshipped a head, that they possessed the Holy Grail, and that they had found the Ark of the Covenant. Thus to anyone studying arcane and esoteric beliefs, the Knights Templar were irresistibly intriguing. Conspiracy theories about them still abound and books about them, from the excitably written *The Holy Blood and the Holy Grail* to the wickedly tongue-in-cheek *Foucault's Pendulum* have proved to be best sellers.

NEWTON, ISAAC

Sir Isaac Newton (1642 – 1727) is not just one of the giants of science and mathematics. He was also an alchemist and philosopher. He translated the so-called Emerald Tablet, which laid down the beliefs of the Hermetic Tradition. With its belief in a state of "oneness" with the divine and nature, it appealed to Newton, who was ultimately to reject the standard belief in the Trinity, and become a Unitarian. He also took an interest in the traditions of the Jewish religion, and devised a method for uniting the chronologies of the Old Testament with "pagan" (i.e. Egyptian, Greek and Roman) chronologies. This theory was important to John Wood, as were Newton's studies of Solomon's Temple.

Many of Newton's discoveries, particularly those about light, came about as a result of his alchemical experiments. It is sometimes said that he was a Freemason. He belonged to the Gentlemen's Club of Spalding, a society not unlike a Masonic lodge. Other luminaries, such as Alexander Pope and William Stukeley, were also members. His Unitarianism he kept secret, for fear of persecution, although he discussed it with Trinitarians such as William Stukeley. However, on his deathbed, he finally refused to accept the Sacrament, an affirmation of his Unitarian beliefs.

PALLADIANISM

Palladianism was more than just a fashion in architecture. As Wood explained in *The Origin of Building*, Palladio looked to nature for the decorations on his buildings – each ornament must be in sympathy with the order of architecture to which it is added. It was another expression of art and nature being at one. To people like Viscount Cobham, who laid out Stowe Landscape garden, Palladianism represented classical reason, and clear Whig thought. Stowe itself was a political statement, using architecture as an instrument of satire. Palladianism was all part of the "Augustan" age, when Greek and Roman writers, artists and architects were regarded as representatives of a Golden Era.

ROSICRUCIANISM

In 1614, John Valentine Andrea, a German monk, published a book called *The Chemical Marriage*, which he claimed was by Christian Rosenkreutz, the third document reputedly by this writer. Almost certainly the other two were also by Andrea, who believed that mankind would be improved through learning. He intended the books to be allegories, not unlike *Pilgrim's Progress*. In the earliest book, *Fama Fraternitatis*, Rosenkreutz travels to the east and studies with Arabs and African philosophers. On his return to Europe he advocates a reform of morals and science. When this is rejected, he and a handful of companions form a secret society dedicated to learning. They build a temple to the Holy Ghost, but when Rosenkreutz is 100 years old he dies, and two of the brethren bury him in a secret place. The society continues for another 120 years, still in secret, with the temple locked. At the end of that time, the temple is opened, and it is found to be the burial place of Rosenkreutz. The story was intended to encourage philanthropy, learning and enlightenment.

Almost immediately the books were misunderstood. People wanted to join the order, but it did not exist. As a result a Dutch alchemical group formed an order called the Rosicrucians in 1622. It established itself quite early in England, and had many influential members. Ashmole was almost certainly one, and Newton also owned Rosicrucian publications. Perhaps the most illustrious Rosicrucian was Sir Francis Bacon. The order is represented by "The Rosy Cross", a combination of a Rose and a Cross. This suggests that it was Andrea who invented the story for he was a Lutheran, and Luther's seal included a rose and a cross.

STUKELEY, WILLIAM

William Stukeley (1687 – 1765) was an antiquarian who, like Ashmole, interested himself in Freemasonry. His interest, however, was born out of his enthusiasm for the Druids. Clergyman and medical doctor, he had an enquiring mind, and in 1717 became a member of the Royal Society, joining the Society of Antiquaries a year later and becoming a Freemason three years after that. In 1724 he began publishing books about the curiosities he encountered on his travels. He had been inspired by the discoveries of the Wiltshire antiquarian John Aubrey, whose studies of Stonehenge and Avebury had fired his imagination. Stukeley was critical of the survey of Stonehenge carried out by Inigo Jones, although his own survey was equally a triumph of imagination over fact.

Stukeley became friends with Sir Isaac Newton in Newton's later years, and wrote a memoir about him. It includes the famous story about the apple as the inspiration for Newton's theory of gravity, which Stukeley claimed he heard from the great man's own lips. However, Stukeley, who became an Anglican clergyman two years after Newton's death, firmly believed in the Trinity, and always refused to accept that Newton held any other than the most orthodox religious beliefs. This may just have been blind prejudice, but it is possible that Newton kept his true feelings secret from him, fearing betrayal.

Although Stukeley was a friend of Newton's, he was no friend of John Wood.

Wood poked fun at Stukeley's survey of Stonehenge. Stukeley made it clear he regarded Wood as an opportunistic plagiarist, although he himself had borrowed Aubrey's ideas. The Society of Antiquaries were eventually to dismiss Stukeley as secretary, because he kept information given to the society for himself, and resented other incomers such as Wood. He denied other members of the Society access to reports and minutes of meetings. Nevertheless, despite his faults, his enthusiasm for ancient monuments and the way in which he studied them make him a significant figure in modern archaeology.

TOLAND, JOHN

John Toland was a man who courted controversy. Born into an Irish Catholic family in 1670, he became a Protestant at the age of 15. This led him to become a freethinker, and he wrote pamphlets on religious tolerance and civil liberties. Tolerance, however, was not a quality extended to him. He wrote a book which said that human reason could explain Christian mysteries. This called down the fury of the church upon his head, and he was constantly at risk of being prosecuted for heresy. In 1705 he declared himself to be a pantheist, but his views on the universe have much in common with Hermeticism. In many ways he was a man far ahead of his time.

In 1717 he set up a neo-Druidic Order (see Druidism) although in his *History of the Druids*, posthumously published in 1726, he portrayed the Druids as unscrupulous mountebanks and theocratic tyrants. This was a rather surprising view for the man who, nine years earlier, had helped to found the Universal Druid Bond and been its first "Chosen Chief." He maintained that no myth had a greater value than another, and his "support" of the Irish Druids may simply have been a way of indicating that these legends were just as worthy to be believed as any Jewish or Christian myth. He also wrote, in the same book, that "ignorance becoming triumphant begets Credulity". His writings were very influential upon Wood, who seems conveniently to have ignored Toland's cynical view of the priesthood.

UNITARIANISM

Unitarianism is a religion based on Christian principles which denies the Trinity, affirming instead the oneness of God. Some Christians, even today, do not accept that they are Christian, especially as they believe that Jesus was not divine, but a great moralist and philosopher. Unitarianism is, in fact, very liberal and open-minded, and Jerom Murch, seven times Mayor of Bath, displayed the industry, philanthropy and cheerful enthusiasm of many Unitarians. The sect, which found a safe refuge from persecution in Poland in the sixteenth century, was already being talked about in this country by the mid-seventeenth century. The first formal Unitarian congregation in England was founded in London in 1774. One of its advocates was the scientist Joseph Priestley, and his writings influenced the reformer Jeremy Bentham. Its appeal to freethinkers, including Samuel Taylor Coleridge, meant that by the late eighteenth century it was regarded with deep suspicion by the government, who saw it as a platform for sedition. Some Unitarians were locked up for their beliefs.

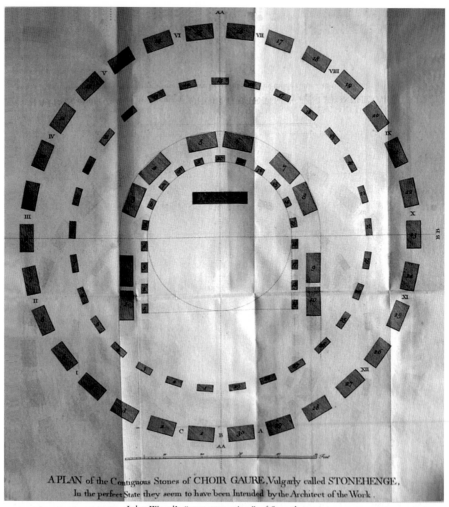

A PLAN of the Contiguous Stones of CHOIR GAURE, Vulgarly called STONEHENGE,
In the perfect State they seem to have been Intended by the Architect of the Work.

John Wood's "reconstruction" of Stonehenge

3 JOHN WOOD – WRITER

John Wood is not just important to Bath because of his architecture. He was also an author. Best known is the *Description of Bath*, or *An Essay towards a Description of Bath*, to give it its full title. This ran to three editions, of which the first, published in three volumes between 1742 and 1743, was radically different from the later editions. It was not, however, his first book. The first to be published was *The Origin of Building*, which has the subtitle *The Plagiarism of the Heathens Detected* (John Wood was not one for short, snappy titles). However, the last to be published was the first to be written. This was his survey of Stonehenge, a book glorying in the stupendous title of *Choir Gaure, vulgarly called STONEHENGE on Salisbury Plain, Described, Restored and Explained in a Letter to the Right Honourable Edward, Late Earl of Oxford and Earl Mortimer*. It was written in 1740, but not published until 1747.

It is in this book that today's reader gets closest to the real John Wood. He is as prickly, self-justifying and at times downright irritating as he is in the other books, but we get glimpses of the man and his family life which are never revealed elsewhere. This is a man who has already experienced disappointment, but still believes that he is going somewhere. Although the title and some of the flowery compliments sound almost servile to our ears, especially when he signs the letter "I am, my lord, your lordship's most humble and most obedient servant", he writes in the main part of the book as if to an equal. The style fluctuates between the grandiose and the chatty. The opening is worthy of Shakespeare. "Caesar! Even Julius Caesar … undeniably proves the Britannick Island to have been enriched with the Great School of Learning and the only school … where the Druids could perfect themselves in their profession." Later we hear about a range of colourful characters, who leap from the pages. At his best, he can be compulsive reading.

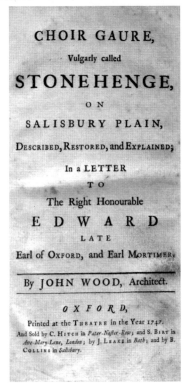

CHOIR GAURE,

Vulgarly called

STONEHENGE,

ON

SALISBURY PLAIN,

DESCRIBED, RESTORED, and EXPLAINED;

In a LETTER

TO

The Right Honourable

EDWARD

LATE

Earl of OXFORD, and Earl MORTIMER.

By JOHN WOOD, Architect.

OXFORD,

Printed at the THEATRE in the Year 1747.
And Sold by C. HITCH in *Pater-Noster-Row*; and S. BIRT in *Ave-Mary-Lane, London*; by J. LEAKE in *Bath*; and by B. COLLINS in *Salisbury*.

We hear about John Wood the Younger, whom he takes to help him in the survey at Stonehenge and "to imprint on the mind of my eldest son and chief assistant the strongest ideas of accuracy in this his first practical lesson of surveying." The boy was just thirteen at the time. He mentions his asthma in passing. Living at Stonehenge, in a little hut, was an old carpenter known as Gaffer Hunt. Wood and Hunt got on like a house on fire, but it seems that Gaffer Hunt's little hut was very smoky. Wood encountered a number of inconveniences on the site and "Sitting in Gaffer Hunt's little smoky hut in the body of the ruins to protract and delineate on paper the several parts of the work as I measured them, to dine and to rest myself were not the least, as I want breath to rise from my chair when I am once settled in."

Another episode gives us a view of the architect with which we are unfamiliar – quick thinking in an emergency that allows him to get out of a possible scrape in an amusing way. Following a storm of sleet and snow, some of the bystanders feared that he had aroused devils, for it was only October. However, Wood tells us, the only devils were living demons in the shape of idle people coming from Weyhill Fair. Two of them showed clear signs of having been in a fight elsewhere and John Wood

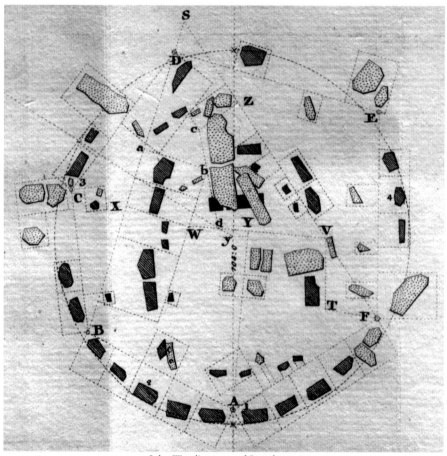

John Wood's survey of Stonehenge

realised too late that they had their eyes on his horses and his watch, which he had unwisely removed from his pocket while they were standing nearby. Indulging in what must have been some very smooth talking, he persuaded them to stand further away to act as points from which he could take survey readings. And with that he sent them off to the furthest extent of Stonehenge – well away from his valuable property. Another and more welcome visitor was Lady Frances Hanbury Williams, who seems to have been highly entertained by Wood's painstaking efforts.

Comparing this photograph with the survey on the previous page, it can be seen how accurate Wood's work was. (The block of stones at the bottom of the survey are to the right in this picture.)

The book also reveals a certain dichotomy in Wood's character. At one moment, he is poking fun at earlier surveyors of Stonehenge, saying "the Stonehenge they describe is a work that exists only in their imagination." In this he was quite correct. Inigo Jones's survey of 1655 looks impressive, but places the inner stones in a circle. John Aubrey, who visited Stonehenge at about the same time, produced a more closely observed study, and it was he who noticed the depressions around the outer rampart of Stonehenge, which now bear his name. It was John Wood's bugbear, Dr William Stukeley, with his surveys over the period 1721 – 1724, who fired up the architect to go and look for himself. As Wood explained scornfully, Stukeley made statements about the area and circumference of the circles without having an understanding of π, the factor crucial to anyone dealing with circles. Stukeley had, of course, been critical of Inigo Jones's survey, and since Jones was something of a hero to Wood, he was determined to sort the matter out to his own satisfaction. Having done so, he found that not only was Stukeley wrong – so was Jones. This first true survey of Stonehenge is, tragically, almost forgotten today, and it is Stukeley who has grabbed the limelight. Yet compare Wood's survey with a modern survey, and one can see how brilliant and how accurate it was. However, having carried out this wonderful piece of work, John Wood then embarked on some extraordinary flights of fancy about the history of Stonehenge, concurring with Aubrey and Stukeley that it was the Druids who built it. Not only that, but he managed to link it with his legendary hero Bladud and with classical architecture, stating that once upon a time the stones had been beautifully cut, before weathering to their current rough state. This may have been an attempt partially to vindicate Jones's work, although Wood felt that Grecian refugees, who had come to Britain with Bladud, might have been responsible for building Stonehenge Much of this work on Stonehenge reappears in the *Description of Bath*.

In Wood's second book *The Origin of Building* published in 1741, we get more of his strange theorising about history. He was, however, following in the footsteps of earlier writers, notably Isaac Newton. He was clearly familiar with Newton's works on chronology and Solomon's Temple and one question which remains to be answered is how he knew them as they were published posthumously in 1728, by which time Wood was already in Bath. Did he or one of his friends or patrons have a copy of Newton's works? There is the remote but exciting possibility that he knew Isaac Newton. Many puzzling aspects of Wood's wide-ranging and esoteric knowledge would fall into place if this were the case. It would also explain the personal nature of the antagonism between Stukeley and Wood, especially if Wood were made privy to secrets which Stukeley was not.

The most fascinating aspect of *The Origin of Building* is that the Reference Library at Bath has both the manuscript and the final printed versions. This allows comparisons to be made between Wood's first ideas and the final version. They are radically different, with great chunks of the draft failing to make an appearance.

The first question which arises is the matter of the handwriting in the manuscript. The first draft is written in a very neat (but difficult to read) script on the recto or right hand pages. Amendments, sometimes in red ink, appear on the recto pages but insertions have been put on the verso or left hand pages. At first glance the writing appears different, and it has been suggested that the handwriting of the main text is that of a secretary, and not John Wood's. However, while there are differences, there are also some striking resemblances. The angle of the writing is the same in both hands. Looking at the lower case letters, the stroke of "t" in both hands is very tall, and almost without a cross. Sometimes the cross does not appear at all. The "i"s are all dotted very meticulously over the letter and at the same distance. The loops on "f" are identical, and another idiosyncrasy that occurs in both hands is that the tails on "g" and "y" at the end of words are standard italic arcs, but within the word are often translated into loops. Turning to capital letters, B D R and P in the neat version are usually copybook letters with serifs but as the writer becomes more involved with the text they convert to being written with loops as in scribbled hand. Most characteristic are the capital Zs, which are identical in both hands. All in all, it seems a fair assumption that the recto pages are John Wood's neat handwriting while the other hand is Wood writing in a hurry or in excitement. There is further confirmation of this on a deed in Bath Record Office, signed by John Wood, on which the same neat handwriting occurs on the plan. To hold in one's hands a book to which Wood has added contributions is interesting enough, but to hold an entire book in Wood's own handwriting is an experience both exciting and moving.

Example of verso and recto pages

Whatever the truth behind the writing, the manuscript version gives an insight into Wood's thought processes as he traces the history of architecture back to Adam and Eve's expulsion from the Garden of Eden. The heathens of the subtitle, whose plagiarism is detected, are the Egyptians, Persians, Greeks and Romans, all of whom, Wood asserts, owed their building skills to the Jews. This immediately puts him on a collision course with the Roman writer Vitruvius, who not unnaturally had a different view of the origins of architecture. Thus even he is given the occasional rap over the knuckles. Generously, Wood allows that it is not Vitruvius's fault that he had the wrong ideas, but that of Augustus. Vitruvius, he kindly acknowledges, wrote his books on architecture at a time when Augustus was consulting the Sybilline books and as he burnt 2000 volumes "can there remain the least doubt that Vitruvius attributed to the Grecians what should have been attributed to the Jews?" As Vitruvius inspired another of Wood's heroes, Palladio, an explanation of this sort was clearly necessary.

Isaac Newton, however, remains almost untouchable. In Book IV, Wood needs to prove that Sesostris, King of Egypt and Rehoboam, the son of Solomon, were contemporaries, for his theory of the origin of architecture to work. He starts out boldly enough by explaining how apparently contradictory chronologies can be made to agree, by using Newton's method of dating. Bit by bit, as he gets into ever deeper water, the writing gets smaller and smaller, and the crossings out become more frequent until he is forced to admit that it appears that the Fall of Troy must have occurred after the date given by Newton. Newton's chronology appears to be wrong and hence Wood's elaborately constructed theory collapses in ruins. By the printed version, however, with one bound he is free of this apparent impasse. He drags in Herodotus "the only historian of all antiquity, before Diodorus Siculus, that had his account from the Egyptian records". After some very dubious arithmetic, he concludes triumphantly that "Rehoboam and Sesostris were contemporaries: and by consequence Sesostris was the King of Egypt who invaded Rehoboam and spoiled the temple of Jerusalem, in the fifth year of his reign." His relief is palpable.

The writing gets smaller and the crossings out more frequent

Numerology plays a large part in this section, and several numbers have special qualities for him especially the "remarkable number seven". Some pages have figures scrawled on them as Wood struggles to establish the length of the cubit. At first he decides that the cubit is 18inches and $\frac{49\frac{1}{2}}{83\frac{1}{3}}$ of an inch. (Quite why he chooses to express it like this is a puzzle. 297/500 would be a simpler way of putting it.) Later he wrestles with various other versions of the cubit, and further complicated long multiplication and division sums appear. To follow someone's mental processes in this way brings them very close indeed.

The printed edition is a much tighter book – one wonders who persuaded Wood to cut great swathes of the original, including the tactless remark about previous histories. Missing from the final version are his suggested improvements for the King's Bath. Although the omission makes sense – the plans appeared in a section dealing with the building of Noah's Ark – it is frustrating that we only get a description of his plans without the projected illustrative plates. Wood admits in the manuscript that it is a digression, and apparently decided later they were a digression too far.

As ever with Wood, the book is more readable when he is dealing with practicalities. The endless Biblical theorising becomes tedious, though to educated readers of his day this was cutting-edge historical theory. To our ears it is more interesting to know that he considered that every part of creation was circular or of a circular form. To increase perfection it should be possible to divide a circle into three principle parts, which can then be sub-divided into three further parts. The Circus immediately leaps to mind, with its three segments and its three orders of architecture.

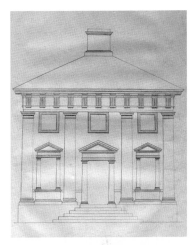

The early chapters of *The Origin of Building* trace the story of architecture from the Jews, who became artificers in bricks and mortar while in bondage in Egypt. As empires rise and fall, and rulers disobey God's law, the gift of architecture moves from the Jews to the Egyptians, then to Assyria, Babylon, Persia, Greece and Rome. Finally, Wood brings story back to Britain with Stonehenge and Stanton Drew.

Of much greater interest to modern readers are Wood's comments on the orders of architecture, illustrated with beautifully detailed engravings. It is here that he refutes the Vitruvian explanations of the orders, and insists that they are based on Jewish motifs. The volutes on ionic columns, for instance, refer to the ram's horns blown as trumpets. Wood dislikes the Greek Ionic order, with the flat volutes, much preferring the volutes which come at an angle. It comes as no surprise to learn that these are extolled by Palladio and used by Inigo Jones. Among the illustrations are his pictures of three "cottages", one to each order. One of these, the Doric order cottage, was finally built for Jerry Peirce, surgeon at the Mineral Water Hospital. Known as Lilliput Castle, it is now lost among the later accretions of the house known as Battlefields, at the northern end of Lansdown.

As Tim Mowl has noted in his book *John Wood – Architect of Obsession* these plans for miniature Palladian houses sit rather oddly in a chapter about Moses' Tabernacle, but the excuse that Wood gives is that he is describing the cottages that the Jewish the workmen built for themselves.

The Origin of Building is one of the books that those who believe Wood was a Freemason put forward as part of their evidence. It is true that he refers to God as "the Great Architect of the Universe" and that, like James Anderson, he traces architecture to Solomon's Temple, but he also makes some notably unmasonic points in the book. First there is the statement in the unpublished introduction that previous accounts are imperfect. This can only be an attack on Anderson, whose book *Constitutions of Freemasonry* was published in 1723. Second, Wood makes no reference at all to a figure beloved by Freemasons, the legendary architect of Solomon's Temple, Hiram Abiff. The omission seems quite pointed for he teasingly mentions King Hiram of Tyre, but later clearly says that God, the divine architect, was responsible for the temple's design. Third, while acknowledging that there are those (and he must mean Anderson) who believe that the three orders of architecture can be traced back to Solomon's Temple, he maintains that at least two of the orders go back further, to Moses' Tabernacle. His plan of Solomon's Temple resembles Isaac Newton's rather than the Masonic image, although Wood's is less cluttered. Simply referring to God as the Great Architect does not make Wood a Freemason. It is a term used by other sects and, indeed, other religions.

The value of *The Origin of Building* – in particular the manuscript version – shows that Wood is not just regurgitating other people's ideas. Instead, with its alterations, excisions and additions, it conveys the struggle of a man who is genuinely trying to make sense of all he has read and learnt, sometimes realizing, to his dismay, that even great men like Newton can be wrong. He is then conveying his conclusions to others.

Wood's most important publication for anyone interested in Bath's history is the *Description of Bath*. The first edition of 1742 is quite a small-scale work, dealing with the history of Bath (as perceived by John Wood) until the time of the Saxons. It was followed in 1743 by a second volume, containing a description of the city in two parts. Together these volumes form the basis for the later, much expanded work. The most interesting book is the third volume, added in 1743. This contains ideas and illustrations that never resurfaced, as Wood's hopes and dreams for the city failed to materialise. They include a proposal for a harbour to make Bath an important inland port, and the master plan for the city, that was already slipping from his grasp. "I proposed," he wrote, "to take an exact plan of the city and after laying out the whole in a regular manner, every person that should take a new lease of any of the Chamber [i.e. Council's] lands and tenements was to covenant to build nothing but what should be conformable to it." Alas, his plans were treated scornfully. Despite offering to lay aside his designs for Queen Square, many councillors remained unimpressed. Although he won over some, others, he wrote angrily, "thought proper to treat my schemes as chimerical." By the second edition of the book, his attempt at town planning had been removed.

It is the second edition, published in 1749, and reissued virtually unaltered after Wood's death, which is the most valuable to historians. In four parts, it not only deals with Bath's history, theories on stone circles and Wood's own achievements in the city, but also tells us a great deal about the way in which the city was run. In part it is a glorification, not only of Wood himself, but also of Richard Nash, whom he always refers to as the King of Bath. It is quite clear at one point that Nash and Wood had collaborated to hoodwink the council over sedan-chair fares, and one is left wondering what other schemes they cooked up. It also raises the possibility that it was Nash who persuaded Wood to drop the attack on James Anderson at the start of *The Origin of Building*. As a Freemason himself, he could hardly have welcomed it.

The first part begins, somewhat unexpectedly to anyone who has not read Wood before, with Dinocrates, the architect of Alexander the Great. Without any hesitation, Wood has leapt into myth-making. In no time at all we are introduced to Bladud, Brutus, the son of Aeneas, and Romulus and Remus. Solomon's Temple makes an inevitable appearance by page 17. Much of what follows is a summary of *The Origin of Building* but all this is mere scene-setting for Bladud, and an attempt to establish that he was king of Britain around 500 BC. Wood finally announces that Bladud is none other than the legendary Abaris the Hyperborean, priest of Apollo, disciple of – or possibly the master of – Pythagoras, and endowed with the gift of prophecy.

We then learn that the city was once in three parts, the central part around the springs, the second part about eight miles to the west at Stanton Drew, and the third part about fifteen miles south at Wookey Hole. This would have made it as large as Babylon, had it not been reduced by the Romans and later by King Alfred. In amongst these fictions, there are some sensible observations on the geology, plants, and above all the springs, both hot and cold. There is also some interesting information about seventeenth century Bath, and the surrounding villages. Many of these also seem also to have had a mystical past. Saltford, we learn, was a village sacred to Apollo, while Tatwick was sacred to Mercury, and Limpley Stoke to Diana.

Part II finds us back with the Druids and Bladud. We will look more closely at Wood's beliefs about these later, for they became increasingly important to him. There seems little doubt that Wood saw himself as a Druid, and perhaps even a second Bladud. Central to his theories were the stone circles at Stanton Drew, and his thoughts on these, together with modern theories about them will be discussed in Chapter 5. So the story moves on, with King Arthur making a brief appearance on Mons Badonca, identified by Wood as Lansdown. This section is a strange mixture of facts, folk tales, and quotes from authors such as John Leland and John Harington. Towards the close of this section he moves on to firmer ground, with a description of Bath in the early eighteenth century. It is from these pages that we get some idea of how Richard Nash shook the city out of its complacency, and persuaded it to bring in much needed improvements. Alas, as Wood tells us bitterly, "this Bathonian sovereign hath often fed those who should have feasted him." Neither man ever received much thanks from the city for which they did so much, and this terse remark is a measure of Wood's resentment.

The second half of the book – parts III and IV – is indeed a *Description of Bath*, or at least a description of the city as it was midway through the eighteenth century. Even here, Mons Badonca, Bladud, and the goddess Diana still manage to make an appearance. Myth is never far away when Wood picks up the pen, though his reporting skills are commendable. This is the section which is so invaluable to historians, with its wealth of detail on a rich variety of subjects – the baths, the charities, the streets, new and old, laws, both statute and honorary, and amusements. We learn about everything from the first treasurers of the General Hospital, to the overabundance of turnspit dogs in the city.

The book ends in most peculiar way. After this wealth of description about Bath, we are suddenly treated to the story of Sylvia, a girl who lost her fortune in gambling, and fell upon hard times. Wood took her into his house (under what circumstances it is not clear, although she paid rent) but while he was away on business she committed suicide. One is left wondering what the relationship was between them. He tells us that when he heard of her death while on his way back to Bath, he took post horses to get home in what seems to have been a terrifying journey.

> Every bush I galloped by looked like an infernal spirit; every large stone and clod
> of dirt that lay in the road appeared like a hobgoblin; and stone walls resembled
> nothing but swarms of dreadful spectres. The rustling of the trees, and the sound
> of the horses feet filled my ears with nothing but the groans and howlings of
> people in the utmost distress.

It seems something of an over-reaction to the death of a woman who supposedly meant nothing to him. Odder still is what happens next. She owed him £52 in rent, so he seizes her belongings and auctions them off, thereby, he tells us proudly, totally discharging the debt.

The last chapter of the book closes with a bizarre ghost story, which happened to a supposed friend, although given some of the scatological detail in the tale, and the sly "nudge nudge wink wink" tone, again one is left pondering just how much of a friend he was. Like all good ghost stories, it ends with a natural explanation for the spectral happenings. Wood, for all his belief in Druids, and his fearful imaginings as he rides back to Bath after Sylvia's death, is always ready to laugh at other people's credulity. And needless to say, there is a short postscript, which leaves us not at Bath but at Stanton Drew.

People are usually either dreamers or doers. What the books reveal to us above all is that John Wood was both – not just the vigorous and practical man of action who efficiently carried out the first true survey of Stonehenge but also the philosopher who devised an elaborate theological system for the Druids of his imagination. That dichotomy in his character seems to have left him a troubled and dissatisfied man.

Stonehenge – an Edwardian view

SUNRISE AT STONEHENGE   COPYRIGHT 21·6·24·

An excited crowd in the 1920s watch the sunrise at Stonehenge

Storm clouds over Stonehenge

Stanton Drew – The Great Circle

Stanton Drew – the Small or North East Circle

Stanton Drew – the South West Circle

Stanton Drew – the red stone

Stanton Drew – one of the limestone slabs

Stanton Drew – "the force runs from east to west"

Stanton Drew – The Cove

Stanton Drew – the Druids Arms

Stanton Drew – the toll-house on the main road

South Parade – "it is nevertheless a magnificent pile"

The Cricket Field where part of the Royal Forum should have been

Queen Square – The Palace Front

The Obelisk – symbol of sun worship

One of the grotesque faces in Queen Square not "drawn from nature"

By comparison, Wood demonstrates a true Palladian grotesque

The auditorium of the Teatro Olimpico in Vicenza

The Royal Crescent – auditorium for the opening celebrations of the Bath International Festival.
Although the orders of architecture are different, the resemblance to Palladio's building is striking

The Circus with its three orders of architecture, crowned with acorns

The sequence at the corner of Brock Street of the crescent moon, a rose, a star, a mysterious bearded head and the sun. Could these be references to alchemy, Rosicrucianism and the Knights Templar?

The Ouroboros circling a rose and the sun

Thunderbolts as portrayed in
emblematic books

Fasces and a wooden club – Roman
and Druid symbols combined

Beehives and a windmill – both from Whitney's Choice of Emblems

Ten Commandments with a sword and a tomb with skull and crossbones – both possible references to the Knights Templar

Next to each other are two oak trees: one flourishing and the other blown over. Is
this a reference to John Wood's life being cut short? The accompanying poem in
Whitney to the fallen tree suggests that it is

Two Newtonian references – a telescope and a ray of light reflected from a mirror

The Janus Head – one face bearded, one not

The white swan – one of the birds of alchemy

More alchemy: Mercury – or Hermes and the ouroboros with the golden bough – mistletoe

And finally - a symbol laden coat of arms and a replacement carving

The confused outline of the Assembly Rooms on their cramped site

4 BLADUD & THE DRUIDS

An opinion hath almost universally prevailed that every thing recorded of Bladud, one of the ancient British princes, the ninth king of our island in the line of Brutus, and the first discoverer of the hot fountains of Bath is mere fable and romance; but none that I know of have yet undertaken to prove it to be so!

So begins *The Essay towards a Description of Bath*. The book is not only a vindication of Bladud but also a vindication of Wood and an explanation of why he failed to build the city he wanted.

Studying John Wood's works, it is possible to see how the legendary founder of Bath, Bladud, became increasingly important to him. At the same time, his interest in the Druids grew, inspired, it seems, by Toland, a writer whose works he knew well. His own religious philosophy changed too. By the time he wrote *The Description of Bath*, the Bath of his imagination had become the centre of a Druid-led Arcadia, ruled by the magician king, Bladud. Although Wood keeps reminding us, and presumably himself, that Bladud was a pagan, his affection for him is apparent. This is more than a glorification of Bath, or an attempt to discredit Stukeley. If he was a follower of Toland or Newton, then what we may have is his coded version of Pantheism or Unitarianism, hidden, like Newton's Unitarianism, for fear of persecution by the authorities.

It was Stukeley who seems to have provoked Wood into justifying the legend of Bladud. Bladud first appears in 1135 in Geoffrey of Monmouth's *History of the Kings of Britain*, a spurious tale which was condemned as fiction by another monk, William of Newburgh, who called Geoffrey "the father of lies". Over the years it had developed into the story of Bladud, the British prince cast from his father's court because of leprosy, who became a swineherd, only to give the disease to the pigs. The pigs, wandering along while Bladud pondered his next move, found some hot mud, which ultimately cured them. Bladud then tried the same treatment and was also cured. Stukeley ridiculed it in 1724, in the first volume of *Itinerarium Curiosum*, calling it a silly fable. Wood must have been incensed. Cunningly, when attacking debunkers of the story, he found a cruel way of getting at Stukeley. In his criticism of those who poked fun at the old legend, he ignored him, instead saying that it was the Earl of Rochester who had made it "a subject for his wit" as had "one Powell" writing in the Spectator magazine. He found another way of getting at him through the Druids. In 1730 Stukeley became Vicar of Stamford in Lincolnshire. Another legend

says that Bladud founded the University there (which actually existed, briefly, in the fourteenth century.) Wood smartly whipped Bladud away from Stamford, declaring that it was a misinterpretation of the name Stanton Drew, and that was where the Druid University was.

Bladud is much more to Wood than the figure of British legend. He equates him with Abaris the Hyberborean, a figure mentioned in one of Plato's dialogues. A priest of Apollo, he can fly, and carries an arrow of prophecy which he gives to Pythagoras. Apollo figures large in Wood's writings, and he believed that the head which we now identify with Minerva, in the Roman Baths Museum, is actually the head of Apollo – a young, beardless youth. Bladud is descended from Brutus, the son of Aeneas, and arrives in Britain after the Fall of Troy (this was another of Geoffrey of Monmouth's fantasies). Among his other attributes he is an astronomer, as was Wood himself, as we find out in the story of Sylvia. John Wood tells us that the two of them used to look through his telescopes at the moon. Did Wood finally come to see himself as the new Bladud? His coat of arms shows crescents and oak trees, and the crest is a wild man with a club and an oak tree. Bladud, however, is no wild man. Stukeley included a romanticised picture of a Druid in his book about Stonehenge but his Druid looks a positive savage compared with the picture of Bladud in *The Description of Bath*, drawn for Wood by the Bath artist Hoare. He even hints that he may be descended, if not from Bladud, then from the early British, for he says that some families in Bath can trace their history back to Celtic times.

The city Bladud creates is vast, with the university at Stanton Drew, a school for harpists at West Harptree, and a man-made cavern at Wookey Hole for secret ceremonies. The river Axe, he tells us, is named after the axes used in these secret ceremonies. Beechen Cliff, which he calls Blakeleigh, becomes the hill Camalodunum, while Lansdown is the legendary Mons Badonca, famous for being the site of Arthur's last stand. In the original Latin the words "Mount Badon" are written Mons Badonicus, but Wood has subtly changed it for his own reasons. He wants it to be the mountain dedicated to the Moon, or goddess Onca. It gets odder still, for having told us the hills of Bath are four in number, Wood promptly enumerates five: the two aforementioned, plus Bannagh or Banner Down, Kingsdown, and Haul Down, or Solsbury. This last he dedicates to the Sun.

All of this sounds so strange to us that it has been dismissed, yet, as Wood makes clear, much of his information was derived from other authorities at the time. These authorities could be equally fanciful. Stukeley may have dismissed Bladud, but he saw the avenues of standing stones – which he called cursuses – as serpentine, snaking their way across the countryside. Far from being the serpents of his imagination they are, as one modern archaeologist has pointed out, almost obsessively straight, except where they have to wiggle their way around a natural feature. Moreover, if Wood was really a disciple of Sir Isaac Newton, there may have been another subtext to these tales. His persistent references to the Sun and the Moon may have a deeper meaning. Newton was an alchemist, and closer study of Wood suggests that he too knew a great deal about the symbolism of alchemy.

Perhaps Wood was trying to build not just the New Troy, but a monument to alchemy. Of course, this may be a new myth, but in the section on the Circus, we shall look at symbolism whose meaning seems to have been overlooked until now.

John Wood's bookplate

Seal used by Jenny Wood's widow and
John Wood (junior)
1st November 1754

Seal used by John Wood
the Younger
4th November 1754

5 STONEHENGE & STANTON DREW

Britain is peculiarly well endowed with stone circles, but only two sites seem to have gripped John Wood's imagination: Stonehenge and Stanton Drew. It is odd that he has so little time for Avebury, which for Aubrey does "as much excel Stonehenge as a Cathedral does a parish church." Wood was well aware of it – it becomes a college for philosophers in his chain of Druid sites. What makes it odder is that Wood was an antiquarian and a far from incompetent archaeologist. As building work progressed at Bath, for example, and strange relics were turned up, Wood was there to describe them. *The Description of Bath* contains a diagram of remains that Wood found beneath the General Hospital (now the Royal National Hospital for Rheumatic Diseases). Inevitably, these discoveries caused Wood's imagination to leap into overdrive, and we also get plans of a Roman Bath and the Roman city, complete with trees, altars, one each for the sun and moon, and a rocking stone. It is, therefore, puzzling that he was not similarly inspired by Avebury.

Avebury – Aerial view of "The Ring".

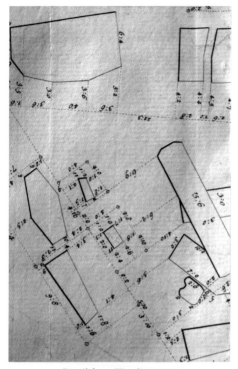
Detail from Wood's survey

Wood's description of Stonehenge, like his Roman city of Bath, is the same mixture of sense and nonsense. Wood's original survey of Stonehenge is masterly. Compare it with a modern survey, and it can be shown that he had even mapped correctly the indentations in the stones. Stukeley, while professing, extremely unctuously, to deplore the fact that he has to disagree with Inigo Jones, produces a proposed layout for the stones in which, to fit the facts, he has had to draw the most complicated series of ellipses, heart shapes and circles, while Jones's earlier survey went for the simplest option – a circle. Neither was correct. At least Wood's projection has the benefit of being the right shape, even if modern techniques show that Stonehenge was built in several stages. His friend and ally, Gaffer Hunt, said no one had conducted a proper survey before, and as a retired carpenter, he knew what he was talking about. He had seen investigators come and go, including Stukeley, and he recognised a proper survey when he saw one. John Wood correctly identifies Avebury as being older than Stonehenge. He has been mocked for saying it was a lunar temple, but the scientist Sir Fred Hoyle put forward the same idea in 1966. It is when Wood starts to speculate about its history that we venture into the realms of fiction, with his chain of Druid colleges spread from Avebury to Exmoor (where the entrails, or exta, were examined.)

In fairness to Wood, it must be said that, even today, there are a myriad of explanations for Stonehenge. A glance at the websites and books devoted to it will verify that. Some are scientific, some are frankly sensational, but the truth is, no one is really any the wiser than John Wood was about the purpose served by Stonehenge. Wood and Stukeley, with their ideas of planetary observatories, are almost in the main stream of modern thinking. But if Stonehenge interested Wood, Stanton Drew was a revelation.

There are two pages in the manuscript version of *The Origin of Building* which show dramatically how excited he was when he discovered Stanton Drew. On the recto page he has written down his theories about Stonehenge, and then, on the verso page facing it, he has written down a lengthy insert about Stanton Drew. One almost has the impression that he has just visited it and has rushed back to jot his ideas down before they get forgotten.

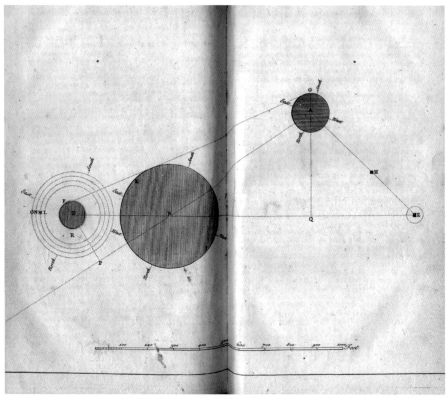

Wood's plan of Stanton Drew from the *Description of Bath*

Visiting Stanton Drew today can be little different from when Wood went. Unlike Stonehenge, it is not commercialised – indeed it is quite hard to find. If you approach the lane from the wrong direction you can easily miss the turning. Leave the car in the small car park which also serves as a turning circle for the houses in the lane, cross a couple fields at the back of a farm, and you are there. The stones mainly lie flat or are tilted at odd angles – only a few still stand upright. In the first field are two circles: the great circle, which requires some imagination to visualise it as it originally was, and the small circle, which is rather more complete. To find the third circle, you have to cross a track, climb a stile, and at the top of a small rise a ring of stones is just visible in the grass. There is no rush of traffic and chatter of tourists, as at Stonehenge – just the sound of wind in the trees and the bleating of sheep. Yet for all its state of decay, it is a most atmospheric place. John Wood was entranced by it. Associated with it is The Cove, - three gigantic stones, one of which has fallen and broken. There is also, on the other side of the valley, a standing stone, now much diminished, known as Hautville's Quoit, which Wood calls Hakill's or Hakim's Quoit. As had happened at Stonehenge, a storm arose, which blew down part of a tree as he began work, intimidating the locals. This was on 12th August, 1740. As ever, in mapping and reporting, Wood is excellent, noting, for example, the three different kinds of stone. Most remarkable is the first one which the visitor sees, for it is of a pronounced red colour, and quite different from the limestone stones near it. This, John Wood believed, came from Wookey Hole. There are also rocks of sandstone. Wood thought he saw the remains of four concentric rings around the smallest circle but it is now known that the stones are not the remains of rings at all, but an avenue to the river. However, he would have been amazed and delighted at the geophysical survey carried out in 1997. This showed no less than nine concentric rings within the Great Circle, and an encircling ditch. It is thought there was a wooden henge here before the stones. Whatever the truth, it appears that the site was as important as Wood kept insisting, although for different reasons.

John Wood saw the layout of the stones as based on the Pythagorean planetary system. Again, he seems to have been not a million miles away from the truth. The most popular theory is that it is a lunar calendar. But inevitably, John Wood could not resist dragging in Solomon's Temple. In the smallest circle, which he saw as a temple dedicated to the moon, he detected the magic sixty cubits, the length of Solomon's temple. However, not only was he beginning to lose interest in Stonehenge, but he was also becoming disenchanted with the temple built by Solomon. He traced the magic figure of sixty cubits back to the temple built under the decree of Cyrus of Persia by Zerubbabel. And here, for the first and only time, he suggests that it might have been circular, although so delicately that, like a magician's trick, it can slip by without the reader noticing, and worded so that John Wood has a get-out clause if challenged. He does not say this was the temple as *built* by Zerubbabel but the temple as *decreed* by Cyrus.

Why should we laugh at John Wood for being beguiled by the magic of Stanton Drew? On my last visit, a small group of Japanese were being taught by a local "expert" that "the force runs east to west, and when the stones are powered up, it acts like an electric fence around the stones." Meanwhile at the southwest circle, another visitor was crouching on each stone in turn, while dangling a crucifix over them. I didn't like to ask to why. Stanton Drew has that sort of effect on people. And even if the experts deny the possibility of the Druid connection, the village does not. The village pub is called The Druid's Arms.

STONEHENGE & STANTON DREW – Some facts and figures

I have used imperial measure rather than metric because that is what John Wood used.

Stonehenge is now considered to have had three distinct construction phases.
Period I c. 2950-2900 BC
Period II c. 2900-2400 BC
Period III c. 2550-1600 BC

The diameter of the outer ring formed by the earth bank is roughly 325 feet and the diameter of the ring of Sarsen stones is 108 feet.

Stanton Drew is thought to have been built between 2600–2500 BC.

The diameter of the Great Circle is 368 feet, of the South West Circle roughly 144 feet and of the North East Circle 97 feet.

These measurements compare with John Wood's works in Bath as follows:

- The Circus has a diameter of 318 feet. The central area has a diameter of 187 feet but this is irrelevant as the garden is of a later date. Grimm's illustration of 1773 just shows the reservoir in the middle, as do maps of the period.

- Queen Square is 316 feet from North to South, 306 feet from East to West. The garden is a square of 206 feet.

- Royal Crescent is 538 feet across.

60 cubits is between 93 and 98 feet depending on the cubit used. Wood was not consistent in his use of cubits, selecting the version that made the figures fit most closely to his theory.

PART TWO
JOHN WOOD IN BATH

1 A MAN WITH A PLAN – SOUTH PARADE

As we stand on South Parade and gaze southwards towards Beechen Cliff, over a very unsatisfactory car park towards the modern blocks of the police station and offices, we are unwittingly looking at the memorial to shattered dreams. When John Wood returned to Bath in 1727, he was bearing with him a plan of the city which he had requested while in Yorkshire, in order to draw up some blueprints for new buildings. His head was full of ideas about the Roman heritage, not to mention the city's earlier, British, history, and he was keen to make his mark. What do we know of this young man, who came bustling into Bath, ready to change the face of its architecture? The answer is – not very much.

Was he a Bathonian? The evidence is inconclusive. Until comparatively recently, most books said that John Wood was born in Yorkshire. All that was known about his birth was that he was in his 50th year when he died. He could have been born as early as June 1703. Then researchers discovered that John Wood, the son of George Wood, believed to be a builder, was christened in St James's Church in Bath on August 23rd 1704. The link is tenuous – John Wood is hardly an uncommon name – but circumstantial evidence shows that this story is probably true. Not only that, but there are hints in his writings that he is local. Here and there, when speaking of the local accent, he says "we, in Somerset". He speaks of "My countryman Tom Coryat of Odcombe". A sentence to be found in the *Description of Bath* runs as follows:

> However, to be a town's born child of the place, descended from a parent whose origin in the city is beyond any memorial, is still reckoned, by some, as the greatest honour an inhabitant can enjoy.

This sounds convincingly like a Bathonian voice – but in a different tone of voice it can be read as a veiled attack on parochialism.

One of his plans which was never realised was for the Ham, where, he declared, the British Forum had been. Here he wanted to construct a new forum, based on the Roman style, but with an "Octangular Basin" as the centrepiece, which would serve as a port for Bath. Opening up the river in this way would have been a mammoth task, but the result would surely have been worth the effort. In Volume III of the first edition of the *Description of Bath* he tells us his views on promoting trade and on market areas. There were games among Grecians to promote trade, he says, while in Roman times a forum was a spacious area surrounded with galleries and benches. These market areas were specialised with a boarium for the sale of animals,

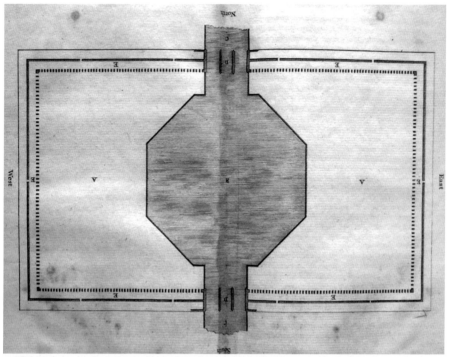

The "Octangular Basin" intended by Wood as a harbour for the city of Bath. Also shown are the surrounding buildings on each side of the river linked by bridges.

a piscarium for the sale of fish and a vinarium for the sale of wine. However, a forum was not just a market Here the people would have celebrated their feasts and festivals as well as carrying on their commerce. By the seventeenth century the Ham was where, on Shrove Tuesday, whole families would go for the "barbarous practice of throwing at cocks". Stones were thrown at live cockerels, which each family provided. Wood planned to restore it to what he felt were its former glories, and his forum would be grander than the Roman one. As well as the port there were to be colonnaded piazzas on each bank with bridges spanning the river. It was to have "an air of magnificence, equal to anything of its kind." It was to be called The Royal Forum – and it was the first of Wood's plans to fall by the wayside. By 1749, the Royal Forum was reduced to being a spacious area for ever to lie open and void. South Parade was built to overlook it, "and though it falls far short of the original design," wrote John Wood, wistfully, "it is nevertheless a magnificent pile."

From South Parade, we can see Beechen Cliff, part of the hill that he calls Camalodunum, blithely ignoring the fact that Colchester is claimed to be Camalodunum. We may also catch a glimpse of Prior Park, another Wood scheme that ended with him at loggerheads with its owner, Ralph Allen. Effectively Wood was finally thrown off the site by Ralph Allen as the two fell out over Wood's grandiose but hardly cosy palace. There is not a word of this in the *Description of Bath* and Wood describes the palace that should have been rather than the building that was.

2 THE DREAMS CRUMBLE

North Parade

By 1739, when John Wood was employed by the Duke of Kingston to build a new estate, he was aware that his plans were not just slipping from his grasp, but being actively opposed by the corrupt, the opportunistic, the envious and the penny-pinching. Hardly had he and the Duke begun work when a tenant, James Jones, realising, if Wood's plans went ahead, he was going to lose his courtyard on which stood a temporary building, took drastic action. An indenture of Chancery between the Duke and Wood from 1739 describes the outcome:

> In the lease is stated that the Upper Terrace walk was intended to be continued of breadth 15 feet beyond the North of the Yard belonging to the house of James Jones to Abbey Green Street lately called Seagers Alley after the expiration of the lease of the said house and yard and agreed with John Wood for these alterations to be made and whereas, a Room formerly built in a slight manner with thin ashlar walls on the yard and premises above mentioned hath been rebuilt in a substantial manner and widened to the northward so as to make a commodious shop projecting so far Eastward that the Upper Terrace Walk cannot be continued and John Wood now releases the Duke of Kingston from that clause and the shop may remain.

The shop was the Parade Coffee House, known today as The Huntsman pub.

There is, in the Lincolnshire archive office, a plan prepared by Wood in 1730 which shows what the terrace would have looked like, had the Parade Coffee House not been built. It also shows Wood's first drawings for a projected circular building on the Abbey Orchard, which he apparently intended to link with the other side of the river by a bridge. Today, half of the area which Wood knew as Abbey Orchard we call Parade Gardens, while his later development, the Parades, covers the southern half of the ground. It appears that the leaseholder, Humphrey Thayer, for unknown reasons, took fright at the scheme and it was abandoned. In 1739, Wood himself leased the land from the Duke of Kingston and planned the Parades. He originally intended the building to have three sections with the centre looking like "the body of a palace". The description continues:

> These three piles of building were to have been of the Corinthian order. And the middle pile I proposed to adorn with columns and pilasters; but the wings were intended plain. The terrace wall was designed to have been divided into recesses,

with arched heads, to answer the apertures in the fronts of the houses; the advanced parts of the wall I intended to rusticate and crown with a balustrade; and I likewise proposed to place obelisks on the pedestals to answer every break in the front of the building.

Once again Wood's dreams crumbled before his eyes. One of the tenants, probably Ralph Allen, a major shareholder, persuaded the others to demand economies. The ornaments were laid aside, the terrace wall built of rubble stone "to the destruction of a design, which, on paper, hath given pleasure and satisfaction to multitudes, among all ranks of people." This was the second time that Ralph Allen had stepped in to scupper Wood's plans. Allen was too powerful for Wood to make an enemy of him, but he never let him invest in one of his developments again. He

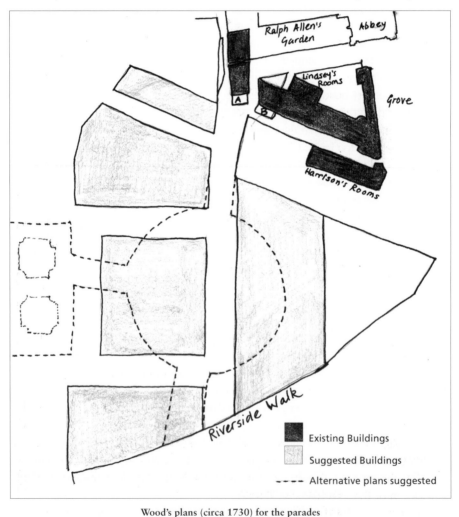

Wood's plans (circa 1730) for the parades
A is James Jones's extension; B is LeonardCoward's shop added in the 1740s
The dotted line suggests his earliest idea was for a circus, but the blocks of buildings show he already
suspected it would be a non-starter

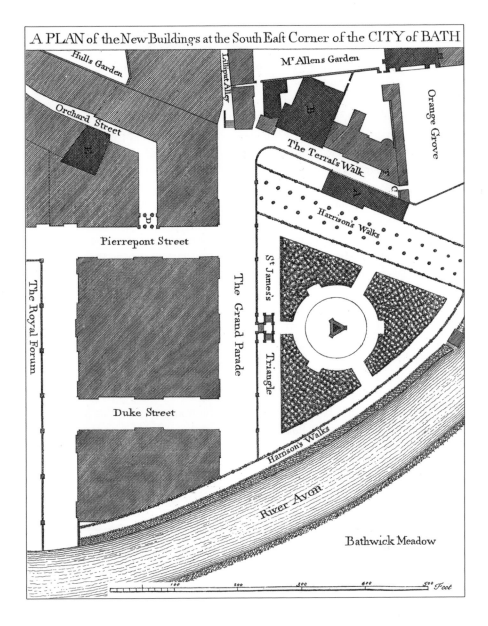

A PLAN of the New Buildings at the South East Corner of the CITY of BATH

Hulls Garden

Mr Allens Garden

Lilliput Alley

Orchard Street

Orange Grove

The Terrafs Walk

Harrison's Walks

Pierrepont Street

St James's

The Royal Forum

The Grand Parade

Triangle

Duke Street

Harrisons Walks

River Avon

Bathwick Meadow

100   200   300   400   500 *Foot*

was forced to redesign the Grand Circus on the Abbey Orchard as a circular garden with an obelisk, but even that failed to materialise, and the circular area became a bowling green.

One development that was built, before Wood fell out with Thayer, was Dame Lindsey's Assembly Rooms. Dame Lindsey, an opera singer, had been a famous beauty at Tunbridge Wells, where she was known as Flavia. Attracted to Bath like so many of Society's hangers-on, she appears at first to have worked as a hostess at Harrison's Assembly Rooms. When John Wood began working in Bath, she persuaded Humphrey Thayer to ask him to design a new set of Assembly Rooms for her, facing the old ones. It is evident from Wood's references to her that he disliked he. This is hardly surprising. She was, to put it bluntly, fairly unscrupulous. It was she who had encouraged the hapless Sylvia in her gambling and then, when Sylvia was almost penniless, employed her to lure young men to the gaming tables.

The new Assembly Rooms, designed so that they "could be turned to other uses for a small expense", opened in 1730 with a public breakfast, at which John Wood unveiled his plans for the Grand Circus on the Abbey Orchard. When Harrison died in January 1735, Dame Lindsey persuaded Nash to let her sister Elizabeth Hayes run his rooms. This was risky, for the two together were quite capable of dubious financial practices, but their ability to work together prevented the rivalry that would afflict the various assembly rooms later on.

Dame Lindsey died in 1736. The rooms were run for a short time by her maid Catherine Lovelace, before another woman, Mrs Wiltshire, took over. She was assisted by her son Walter, who officially became manager on her death in 1747. They were by then known as Wiltshire's Rooms. Eventually competition from the Lower Rooms caused their failure, as Wood seems to have suspected it would, and they were finally pulled down when York Street was built in the early nineteenth century.

York Street

Tucked away at the back of York Street, behind an estate agent's, is the first house that John Wood built for Ralph Allen. (The courtyard is usually kept padlocked but the agents will lend the key out on request.) The house was built as an extension to the old post office where Ralph Allen was postmaster. Long and narrow, with an abundance of decoration, the building is one about which Wood is curiously reticent. So reticent is he, that some people have even doubted that the building is his. Michael Forsyth, writing in the *Pevsner Architectural Guide*, is one who queries the attribution, pointing out not only that that there are no comparable works by Wood, but also that he writes, in the *Description of Bath*, that "the designs, as well as a model for this house were made while I was in London." In other words, it is not clear whether he made the designs or not. But another, easily-missed, extract from the *Description* confirms that Wood did indeed build it.

> While Mr Allen was making the addition to the North part of his house in Lilliput Alley, he new fronted and raised the old building a full story higher; it consists of a Basement storey sustaining a double story under the crowning and this is surmounted by an attic which created a sixth rate house and a sample for the greatest magnificence that was ever proposed by me for our city houses.

The words "by me" give the game away, but this coyness about a piece of his own architecture indicates that he was probably less than happy with its "greatest magnificence". One cannot be certain. He also does not admit outright to building Lilliput Castle, Titanbarrow, and Belcombe Brook Villa, all houses of which he could be, and obviously was, rightly proud. Only the words "Wood Archt." in tiny letters on the plans give the game away. Here, however, there is no plan, and it is likely that

House by Zuccaro

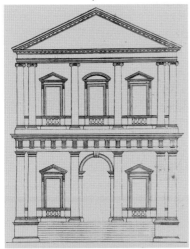

House by Palladio

Titanbarrow by Wood

in his heart of hearts he did not like the house at the back of Lilliput Alley. To discover the reason for his coyness over this building, one needs to turn to two drawings in *The Origin of Building*, which show two houses. The second is designed by Palladio but the first is by an Italian called Federico Zuccaro, one of Palladio's contemporaries. Wood deplores Zuccaro's design, calling his house capricious. Works that are "the products of chance and ignorance or of caprice must offend the eyes and cause abhorrence in the mind," he wrote, and it is Zuccaro's house that he gives as an example. Yet here the proportions and the elaborate decoration are very like those of the villa he despises. Allen must have insisted on the ornaments, which were popular on many early Georgian town-houses in Bath, and the cramped site gave Wood no option but to ignore Palladio's rules of proportion. Small wonder, then, that Wood, for once, is so reluctant to blow his own trumpet.

At this point, it is worth pondering how Wood knew so much about Palladio. In 1721, at the age of seventeen, he was involved in speculative building in London. One year later he was working on the garden improvements at Bramham Park, near Wetherby, in Yorkshire. It is not known who designed Bramham. It may have been the landowner himself, Robert Benson, later Lord Bingley, but it is possible that it was the Italian architect, Giacomo Leoni. Leoni may also have designed a house at Bowden Hill in Wiltshire. It was built for Benjamin Haskin Stiles, for whom Leoni had designed Moor Park House in Hertfordshire in 1720. Stiles fell into debt and the Chippenham house was never completed. The façade then started on its travels, going first to form the front of a clothier's house in Chippenham, and then, in 1933, to the side of a house at Sion Hill Place in Bath owned by Ernest Cook. This façade has often been attributed to Wood, but it is more likely to be by Leoni. This gives two possible Leoni connections to the young John Wood. Furthermore Giacomo Leoni was the Italian architect who produced the first English edition of Palladio. Could the young John Wood have worked for him, or had some contact with him? If Wood was seen as Leoni's artistic heir, this might have been why so many doors opened for him. Leoni had many aristocratic patrons, among them the Dukes of Queensberry and Kent. Although Wood never mentions Leoni, this may be because Wood wanted to be seen as in charge of the situation. Being a mere assistant would not have been a role he relished. It's another question that needs deeper research.

3 A NEW SPA

Abbey Church Yard

As early as 1740, in the manuscript version of *The Origin of Building*, John Wood was voicing his dissatisfaction with the state of the baths. Needless to say, he was ready with plans for their improvement, and gives a full description of them. He had intended adding illustrations but as this section never made it to the final book, we are left trying to imagine what his intentions were. The first plate was to have shown the front of an edifice next to a court of 80 feet square proposed for the King's and Queen's Bath. Another plate was to have shown the principal front and third a building without pillars but embellished with ornaments. He had plans for both King's and Queen's Baths. He proposed:

A Dressing room with slips to be kept warm in winter with hot air or fires and to have dry pumps in each whereby there will be four degrees of heat in the water because each pump would be further from the spring than the next.

A waiting room for servants.

Wet pumps in the baths (that is, pumps where the whole body was soaked, rather than dry pumps, where only certain parts of the body received water, protective clothing supposedly keeping the rest of the body dry.)

A passage round the baths.

A great hall or pump house which was to be a double cube of 33 ft with six pumps for drinking water

A drawing room for gentlemen with WC and an apartment for a person to live in to make coffee, tea etc.

A drawing room for ladies ditto

A house for women bath guides and the same for men guides.

Under the rooms he suggested that there could be a pump for bottling water and for the common people to drink at. Under the Great Hall five slips (that is, entrances via steps) were proposed to be made into the King's Bath with dressing rooms.

None of this was built, and Wood continued with his criticism of the baths in the *Description of Bath*. He complained that the baths filled the bathers with the horror of death. The slips were made of cold stone, wet with steam, dark as dungeons, and without air. The King's Bath was a pit of deformity incrusted with dirt and nastiness, whose annual painting with lime and fine sand made matters worse rather than better. The Queen's Bath was little better, although it was screened from the wind and the prying eyes of spectators. These criticisms are borne out by Tobias Smollett in his *Essay on the External Use of the Water*. However, Wood was possibly being deliberately provocative in the hope of getting his plans acted on. If so, it was not the most tactful way of going about it, and he failed.

Wood also failed to persuade the council to accept his plans for rebuilding the Pump Room. The first one built by John Harvey was condemned as too small almost from the start. Wood tells us that General Wade, MP for the city, supported his plans, but the Mayor, whose son rented Shayler's Coffee House, refused to present them to the council because of fears it would affect his trade. In all his ranting about the injustice of this, which Smollett, for one, would have supported, one has to remember that Wood only tells one side of the story. He is master of presenting the facts as he wishes the reader to perceive them. No doubt the servants were noisy and threw things on to the bathers as they waited to fill their bottles at the common pump, and no doubt there was corruption and dissent among the council members, but Wood is acting as self-publicist here. No other architect, surveyor or councillor is being allowed their say. It would be interesting to know the unvarnished truth behind the controversy.

Anyone standing in the Abbey Church Yard is directly above the Roman Baths and the Temple Precinct. These were discovered the year after Wood died, but he was certain that baths were built originally by the Romans and were buried as the temples collapsed. This was the shrewd John Wood coming to the fore, but his conjectural plan of how he thought the Roman Bath looked is more medieval than Augustan. This is not surprising, for what he took to be Roman remains in the King's Bath were almost certainly Norman. Fact and fantasy are never far from each other in Wood's writings.

Hot Bath & Cross Bath

Wood's complaints did not stop with the King's and Queen's Baths. He was nearly as critical of the baths at the other end of Bath Street. The Lepers' Bath, fed by water from the old Hot Bath, he described as mean, obscure, and small. It was a mere ten foot by eight foot. It was only used by the poor, and was beneath many people's notice. However, both the Woods were interested in the well-being of the poor and the Lepers' Bath was included in his plans. The Hot Bath, Wood says, was more sheltered but presented an abject appearance because of the approaches to it. It was 26 feet long and 15 foot 3 inches wide, with a cross in middle, of whose architecture Wood was very critical. The patients at the new General Hospital had been given the right, by Act of Parliament, to bathe in this bath rather than the Leper's Bath. All of this Wood reports concisely and accurately, only to go on to produce one of the many myths about the waters.

> … unless that right [to bathe in the Hot Bath] should be extended to the other baths, I fear it will bring great disreputation upon the hot waters of the city; it being a truth uncontrovertible, that the water of one bath is improper for that

disease which the water of another bath absolutely cures; and therefore, without the use of the other baths, several patients will be liable to be sent from the hospital, as incurable, without so much as trying the effects of our sovereign waters.

One could forgive him for saying this were it not that doctors such as Tobias Smollett, whom Wood knew, were already discrediting this sort of nonsense. It was his son, John Wood the Younger, who finally rebuilt the Hot Bath in 1777 on its present site, removing the Lepers' Bath in the process.

Wood found the Cross Bath more acceptable. Here people of fashion bathed for pleasure, it being well-sheltered. The bath had a cross in the centre which had been paid for by the Earl of Melfort, after Mary of Modena bathed in it in 1687. Regarded as a popish abomination by the more puritanical townsfolk, it was damaged in 1715 and rebuilt in 1743, when the more obvious Catholic symbolism was quietly removed. It is in Wood's description of bathing at the Cross Bath that we get one of the few chances to see him trip himself up in his story-telling. Writing about the music which was played at the baths, he tells us it stopped in 1676. And that might be that, except that he cannot resist adding a story from Defoe's *Tour thro' Great Britain*, in which he tells us how the musicians played as a young lady entered the bath. Defoe's book was published in 1724, nearly fifty years after the music, was supposed to have stopped.

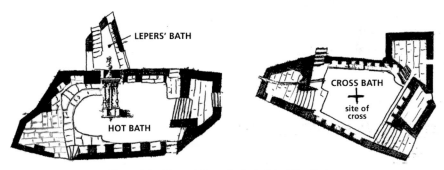

Plans of the Hot and Cross Baths in John Wood's day

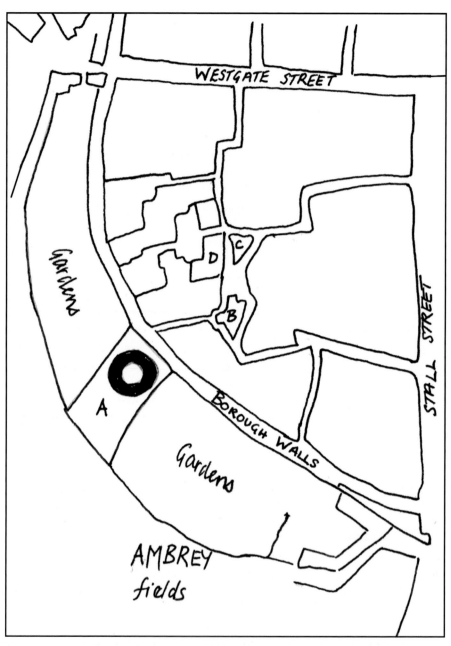

WESTGATE STREET

Gardens

STALL STREET

BOROUGH WALLS

Gardens

AMBREY
fields

Site of Imperial Gymnasium (the first plan for the General Hospital)
as shown on Wood's Survey of Bath 1735
A is the proposed circular building
B is the Hot Bath
C is the Cross Bath

4 FAITH, HOPES & THE CHARITIES

St John's Hospital

In reading Wood's account of his rebuilding of St John's Hospital, there is not a word of the troubles that he faced when working for the Duke of Chandos. Any problems he may have had, he suggests, were due to "another hand, who, by carelessness or incapacity, took such a false survey of the land that there is scarce a right angle in the whole building." We do, however, get some name-dropping reminiscences as he remembers telling the Earl of Oxford "in the presence of my Lord Dupplin" about how important it was for an architect to be well grounded in the theory and practice of geometry. Unfortunately for Wood, the work would have gone a great deal better if he had been grounded in the theory and practice of installing the latest invention, the water closet – but he wasn't. There were constant objections to the smell, which was caused by Wood connecting the down pipes directly into the town sewer. In addition there were interminable complaints from the tenants, who delighted in going behind his back and pouring their woes into the ear of the Duke. Both must have been relieved to see the work complete.

The Mineral Water Hospital

The founding of a General Hospital for the poor had been under discussion since the early part of the century, when Wood was a child in Bath. He must have been excited to have been involved in planning it. Its present site and shape, however, are quite different from what was intended. He was inadvertently foiled in his second attempt to erect a circular building in Bath by the man who had foiled his first attempt – Humphrey Thayer, together with the reluctant landowner, Mr Gay. The land earmarked for the hospital was the Ambrey, just south of the city wall. Wood submitted plans for a "quadrangular" building and a circular one, of about seventy feet in diameter. This was his first real chance at building his "Imperial Gymnasium", which would have had water piped from the Hot Bath into a reservoir in the centre. Since the Hot Bath was close by, the water would still have been hot, and probably at a pleasanter temperature than that in the bath itself. Gay was nervous from the start, objecting first of all that a building "of that sort" would be detrimental to the improvements that were intended for the rest of the estate. Then he heard, via a letter, that one of the trustees was pressing for a building of a hundred feet in diameter. He refused to answer the letter, and it was clear that seventy feet was all he would agree to. Still the plan seemed set to continue. Wood actually drew the proposed building on his map of the City of Bath of 1735. But Thayer, treasurer of the trustees, seems to have been unwilling to part with the money in his care, even when it was needed urgently. It was discovered that the tenant was actually a subtenant. The real leaseholder, Alderman Rosewell Gibbs, was demanding to be recompensed for his surviving part of the lease. While Thayer and other trustees quibbled about this, an opponent of the scheme, who was also a trustee of the hospital, smartly bought the lease off Gibbs instead – and that was the end of the Imperial Gymnasium. Dr. Oliver seems to have been so disgusted that he offered some land himself. However, an Act of Parliament controlling theatres led to the site of the old theatre just inside the walls on the north of the city becoming vacant. In John Wood's words, "the death of Mr Thayer determined the matter in one week's time." In these few words, Thayer's dilatory nature is encapsulated. The building Wood eventually designed is at best competent, and at worst uninspired. Today the General Hospital, having been known for much of its life as the Mineral Water Hospital, is officially known as the Royal National Hospital for Rheumatic Diseases. To local residents it will always be "The Min."

Bluecoat School

One of the most persistent myths about John Wood is that he went to the Bluecoat School. The present Bluecoat School is Victorian, but the original building on the site dated from 1711. Had John Wood gone there, he would have been one of the first children to attend. But almost certainly he did not.

We know how the story started. Rev. John Penrose, visiting Bath in 1766, wrote that the preacher in the Abbey, at a service in aid of the charity schools, said that John Wood "had his education in these schools". As the Bluecoat School is mentioned, everyone has assumed that Wood went there. But the minute books of the school exist from its foundation in 1711, with every child listed. There is no John Wood. Moreover, the children were very poor. Some were even caught begging on one occasion. Assuming we have the right Wood, his father, being a builder, would have been comfortably off. Possibly the family had always been wealthy. One John Wood was Mayor in 1614, while in 1587 another John Wood leased the field in Walcot where the Bell Inn now stands. However, there was another charity school in Bath. It was, of course, King Edward's Free Grammar School. This is a far likelier candidate. His attendance there would explain Wood's knowledge of Latin and mathematics, which has puzzled biographers. Only practical skills were taught at the Bluecoat School. Unfortunately, the records for King Edward's School at that date are missing, but John Wroughton, former headmaster of King Edward's, believes it is possible John Wood went there. He also believes it very likely that John Wood's sons went there.

John Wood put forward a plan for the rebuilding of King Edward's School when a determined headmaster pressurised the council into providing new premises. It was turned down, and the building in Broad Street was designed by Thomas Jelly. Wood makes scant reference to his plans being ignored, and fails to mention that they were a revival of the Imperial Gymnasium scheme. No wonder the council turned it down.

5 PALLADIAN PALACE – QUEEN SQUARE

Nothing sums up better Wood's occasional mixture of fact and convenient fiction than his account of the development of Queen Square. The first fiction is that it is a square – it is not, it is a rectangle, although somewhat less rectangular than Wood first intended. The plan in the *Description of Bath* shows something quite different from what was built. On the south side he planned a wide parade, and the square was to have had three equal sides facing his palace front.

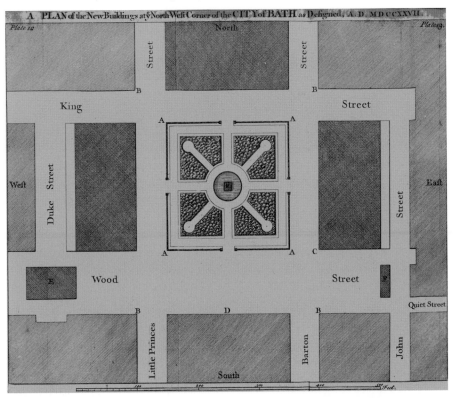

A PLAN of the New Buildings at ÿ North West Corner of the CITY of BATH as Designed, A. D. MDCCXXVII.

Despite its palatial appearance, most of the houses in the square were intended to be lodging houses. Wood was forthright about the conditions of lodgings in the city in the early part of the century. The floors were brown, coloured with soot and small beer to hide the dirt. If the walls were panelled at all, the panelling was unpainted, mean and dirty. Hearths and chimney-pieces were made of whitewashed freestone, and their annual painting left the floors speckled with white paint. The doors were thin with iron fittings, the furniture was cheap and made of oak, and the chairs were cane- or rush-bottomed. Furnishings were also made of cheap materials such as Kidderminster stuff, with bed-linen of dimity or fustian, which the matrons and daughters of the lodging-house keepers embroidered with gaudy wool. In season, the rooms cost ten shillings a week with an extra five shillings for a garret for the servants. The price was halved out of season.

After the improvement in standards pushed through by the new wave of building, the floors were deal or dutch oak boards with carpets. There was fine painted panelling, and the hearths and chimney places were made of marble. The doors had brass locks and the furniture was of walnut and mahogany. The chairs had seats of leather or damask. The prices were naturally higher, and out-of-season reductions less generous. Garrets were as good as rooms for gentlemen were before.

This "before and after" description sounds exactly like a prospectus advertising for investors in a new and exciting development – which is almost certainly what it was. Wood needed investors. But they sometimes had ideas of their own, and since they were paying the piper, they called the tune. On the western side of Queen Square Wood says rather coyly that he found himself "under a necessity of dispensing with a uniform building". The necessity was that two investors, Sir John Buckworth and Mr Grevile, decided they wanted to live in something grander than a terrace. Wood was forced to construct what looked like three great Palladian villas on this side, two at each end, with the middle one set back. There were actually eight houses on this side – three in each of the end villas, the northernmost of which was later entirely owned by Dr. Oliver as lodging-houses, and two, for his recalcitrant investors, in the villa set back.

In the southwest corner he built a chapel for the residents in the square. A curious myth has grown up about this chapel. Almost every book you open insists that it was modelled on Inigo Jones's chapel of St Paul's in Covent Garden. Just one look at pictures of the two shows that this is clearly not the case. The only resemblance is the porch with four columns, and even here there are notable differences. It is clear that, having built three Palladian villas, Wood turned once again to Palladio for the church, and

St Paul's Covent Garden
Architect Inigo Jones

St Mary's Queen Square
Architect John Wood

Il Redentore
Architect Andrea Palladio

St Mary's owed far more to San Giorgio Maggiore and Il Redentore in Venice than it did to St Paul's in Covent Garden.

Another investor, Richard Childs, gave Wood problems on the east side. Two of the doorways have grotesque carvings which must have been shrieking "Zuccaro" at Wood every time he looked at them. Even Zuccaro, who designed a house where the doors and windows are each surrounded by a gaping mouth, might have disapproved of these grotesque faces. It may have been as a reproach to Childs that Wood put a Palladian grotesque over the doorway of the corner house. Could this even be a portrait of the exasperated Wood himself? Perhaps not – though it would make an attractive story.

Finally we turn to the gardens, now sadly over-supplied with unsuitably large trees. Wood carefully planned formal gardens, with an obelisk in the centre, surrounded by a pool. Richard Nash paid for the obelisk, and Wood persuaded him that the correct shape of an obelisk was a tall thin pyramid going directly to a point without being chamfered at the top, as

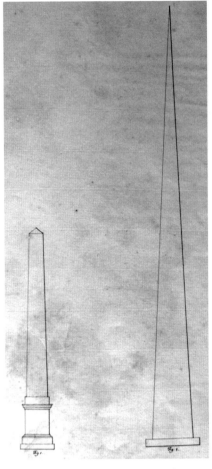

Nash's previous obelisk in Orange Grove had been. It represented, Wood said, a ray of the sun. Unwittingly, Nash had been manoeuvred into supplying the architect with his first symbol of sun worship. The sun and moon were to play an increasing part in Wood's plans for the city. Apollo and Onca were to have their temple returned to them by their Druid acolyte. Unfortunately, Britain, with its unpredictable weather, is not the ideal place for an Egyptian obelisk, and it lost its top in a storm. It now has a chamfered top.

6 FATHER & SON – ROYAL CRESCENT

Wood the Younger, who built the Royal Crescent, faced a continual economic struggle, as the country lurched from boom to bust, from peace to war and back again. Thus the development which began with the Circus in 1754 was only completed twenty years later. We are left with the question – did John Wood the Elder design the Royal Crescent, was it wholly and solely his son's idea, or was it a joint venture? There are indications that Wood the Elder planned a crescent. Tobias Smollett in *Humphrey Clinker*, tells us so. Moreover, there is Wood's obsession with the sun and the moon. He suggested that Stonehenge and Stanton Drew were connected with moon worship, and he studied the moon through his telescopes. He believed that a group of large stones on Lansdown was a Temple to the Sun, standing on a hill dedicated to the Moon. If indeed he was planning to return the city to what he saw as its tutelary deities, then the Circus and the Crescent begin to look very like their temples.

In the new *Pevsner Architectural Guide to Bath*, published in 2003, Michael Forsyth suggests that the Woods were inspired by the colonnade surrounding the auditorium of Palladio's Teatro Olimpico in Vicenza. No one seems to have made this link before. Certainly, standing in the Crescent and looking out over Bath is like looking at a stage set. Moreover, Scamozzi, who also worked on the Teatro Olimpico, was one of Wood the Elder's favourite architects. Another influence on its shape may come from Solomon – not his Temple but his Palace, where the throne room was said to be semicircular. The crescent has been described as elliptical, but it is really more of a squashed semicircle than a true ellipse. It has had many imitators in Bath, although, as Michael Forsyth has observed, its importance elsewhere has been perhaps overstated. It has also been criticised for being chilly and for lacking in ornamentation. If it were intended as a moon temple, then chilliness would be appropriate, although its coldness and severity has been accentuated by the removal of glazing bars in the nineteenth century. Its proportions have been destroyed, sacrificed to the fashion in window-lengthening. If some wealthy philanthropist ever wants to make a contribution to British architecture, then restoring the fenestration on the Crescent should be high on the list of nominated projects. Meanwhile, those who criticise its lack of ornamentation appear oblivious to two facts: first, the Ionic Order does not normally have ornaments, as can be seen from Wood's Ionic Order cottage on page 27; second, if they had been added, any carvings would have to be gigantic, to be in proportion with the Giant Order columns. It would look distinctly odd.

If the Royal Crescent is indeed the temple to the Moon, then it is time to visit the temple to the Sun, to Bel Apollo, and with it to reach the Grand Finale of the walk.

7 THE GRAND FINALE – THE KING'S CIRCUS

All the mythical themes in which John Wood believed come together in the King's Circus. As we have seen, he was desperate to build a circular building. Not only do we have the three orders of architecture he described in *The Origins of Building* but we have other mysterious threads as well. We have the carved metopes with their wide variety of themes and styles. We also have the crowning ring of acorns. Unfortunately, it is not only John Wood the myth-maker who is at work here. Many other people have come up with myths of their own. This would be acceptable if myths were accepted as merely theories, but some, by continual repetition, have become "facts", thus obliterating other equally possible theories.

Let us begin with the facts.

On 11th February 1754, the local paper contained this report.

Last Thursday John Wood Esq laid the first stone towards an intended building which is going to be erected in the field on the north side of Queen Square. It will be called the King's Circus and be about 310 feet in diameter.

It was his final attempt at a circular building. He was never to see it completed. Just over three months later, on Monday 27th May, this notice appeared in the paper.

Last Thursday morning, about three o'clock, died, after a long illness, in the 50th year of his age John Wood, Esq., one of his Majesty's Justices of the Peace for the county of Somersetshire, celebrated for his designs, plans and skill in architecture; more particularly those in this, and a neighbouring city, the second great mercantile trading city of this kingdom. All which is known to be the effect of his great genius, as well as indefatigable study and application in this very noble and useful science. Amidst a world of calumnies, falsehoods and discouragements which he bravely surmounted; he not only raised himself in the esteem of his superiors; but in the compass of a few years, by an honest and commendable industry, obtained a handsome competency for himself and family. In a word he had no enemies but those who either envy'd him themselves, or went too far in crediting the defamatory reproaches and scandal of others.

His dream was unfulfilled. The defiant tone of the obituary suggests that Wood may have written it himself in anticipation of his death. Alternatively, it is possible that it was an angry outburst from a son who felt his father's genius had been neglected. John Wood the Younger was quite capable of fighting talk when the mood took him.

However, we have already slipped into the world of speculation rather than fact.

Although work began on the Circus in 1754, it was not completed until 1769. In 1756 Britain declared war on France. Recession ensued, and work stopped, not resuming until about 1760, with the first, southwest segment still in the process of being built. Considerable preparation must have been needed before building work could start, for the platform on which the Circus stands is artificial, created by large-scale earth-moving. At the same time, considerable effort went into creating the reservoir in the centre, fed by springs. Plans drawn up in 1768 show twelve lease-holders in the southeast segment and ten in the southwest segment, of which one, William Pitt, had a double-width house, now divided into two. There were just six lease-holders in the northern segment, Andrew Sproule of Batheaston having taken a lease on no less than five. He also leased some houses in Brock Street.

These, then, are the facts. It is with the extraordinary façade and its wealth of detail that the myths begin. It has been said that this shows Wood's dedication to Stonehenge, to the Druids, and to Freemasonry, with its connections to Solomon's Temple. Certainly the Circus is a stone circle, and its diameter of 318 feet is not far from being 325 feet, the diameter of the outer earth bank at Stonehenge. What it emphatically is not, as it has been declared to be, is sixty cubits. Sixty cubits was the magic figure which formed the connection between Solomon's Temple, the later Temple by Zerubbabel, Moses' Tabernacle, Stanton Drew – and Freemasonry. By whatever measure you use, sixty cubits is no more than about 100 feet. The Circus is in the region of 200 cubits – which appears to relate to nothing in particular.

One of the most persistent myths about John Wood is that he was a fervent Freemason. At times this appears to be the case. There are, as we shall see, many seemingly Masonic symbols on the Circus. Unfortunately there is no record of Wood being a Freemason, and although the United Grand Lodge of England has searched extensively, no record has turned up of his joining a lodge anywhere. This does not mean he was not one. Many early lodges objected to the formation of the first Grand Lodge, and simply refused to join. The lodge in Bath to which Beau Nash belonged was just such a one. However, we have the list of its members and Wood is not among them. It is possible that he might have become a Freemason while in Yorkshire. His patron, Robert Benson, later Lord Bingley, was a Grand Master of the York Lodge in 1707. This lodge bitterly resented the London lodges and set up a rival Grand Lodge. Alternatively, Wood might have joined a London lodge. It is tempting to choose the Cheapside lodge, now the Globe Lodge. It was an early lodge, formed in 1723, while Wood was in London and it met at the Half Moon tavern. Its symbol was a crescent. The link with Wood is obvious. Unfortunately, its early records are missing. So Wood might still have been a mason, were it not that his *Origin of Building* appears to be an attack on James Anderson, one of modern Freemasonry's founding fathers. Moreover, modern Freemasons say he just does not sound like a Freemason. Freemasonry has an emphasis on sociability whereas Wood was something of a loner. This is not to say he did not have friends, but it is hard to imagine him dining out with a group. They see him simply as an antiquarian with an interest in Freemasonry.

So what is the King's Circus about? It certainly shows the three orders of architecture as described in the *Origin of Building* – Doric, Ionic, and Corinthian. The lowest level is sometimes described by architectural purists as Tuscan. John Wood would be furious. He regarded Tuscan as a debased order, devoid of the proper ornaments. In order to create his relentlessly repeated set of pillars, Wood had to jiggle the proportions slightly. A Doric column, from base to top of the capital, should be eight times its diameter, an Ionic column nine and a Corinthian column ten. It was impossible to set the three orders on top of each one and make them all the same height, especially as he would have needed to start each of the upper

columns with a diameter less than the diameter at the top of the one below it. There was absolutely no way the mathematics would fit. So, despite all his strictures on how important proportion is, he has to cheat – and with a bold combination of slimming down and shortening columns he gets away with it – just.

Around the top of the King's Circus is the ring of acorns. Usually explained to tourists as being a reference to the story of Bladud and the pigs, it is more likely to be a reference to Bladud and the Druids. By 1754 both Woods were using an oak tree and a Druid as personal symbols. Worship of oak trees was at the root of Druid culture. The word Druid may even derive from a Gaelic word meaning oak. Mistletoe, the Golden Bough of myth and legend, often grew on oak trees. The ring of acorns also looks like a crown. Here father and son are surely declaring their belief in the Arch-Druid Bladud, King of Britain.

It is, however, with the carvings on the metopes of the Doric order frieze that we venture into very strange waters indeed. It has long been recognised that some of the carvings were based on emblems in a book by a seventeenth century poet called George Wither. However, the Internet has made other books of emblems widely available, and a search through some of these has revealed sources for many other carvings. It has also revealed that Wither simply copied many of his emblems from these earlier books. Some of the carvings on the Circus are not in Wither at all, but are in emblematic books such as *The Mirror of Majesty* by H.G. and Geoffrey Whitney's *Choice of Emblems* published in 1586. Wither borrowed freely from this book while Whitney, in his turn, had borrowed from the very first emblem book by Andrea Alciato. Some of the emblems which do not occur in Wither are the windmill (from Whitney) while the thunderbolts come from the *Mirror of Majesty*. All the beehives which figure on the Circus come from Whitney's book. There are, however, some emblems which appear to relate to something very strange indeed, but when the Circus and the Crescent are considered together, it suggests that they are not there by accident. It is alchemy.

A frequently recurring theme in the carvings in the Circus is a snake, in many cases forming a circle, with its tail in its mouth. This is a very ancient symbol, and it is called the Ouroboros. It occurs in religions all over the world, but to alchemists it represented the philosopher's stone. It also represented Hermes. Another repeated symbol is the sun – sometimes the ouroboros and the sun occur together in one symbol. Wood had already used this in the altarpiece at Tyberton Church, which he designed for William Brydges in 1727. This wonderful piece of work has many symbols which are also said to represent Freemasonry, much to the frustration of the present vicar, who points out that they are Christian. Most of them are, with the exception of the sun, snake and triangle. They sit rather uneasily on a Christian altar. The sun and moon, Wood's recurring themes, are central to alchemy, and represent gold and silver.

On the corner of the southwest segment of the Circus, by Brock Street, we have a carving of a crescent moon with a face, then one with stars, and then, a little further on, a blazing sun. All of these carvings come from an alchemical emblem book. It can be no coincidence that these occur just as you leave the temple of the sun and head for the temple of the moon.

This all sounds so bizarre that it seems hardly credible. However, once the alchemical theme is discovered, it shrieks at us from every part of the Circus. There is a wolf howling at the moon. The wolf symbolises antimony, the substance Newton used in his alchemical experiments. There are rays of light, another link with Newton, as is the telescope. There is a phoenix, a swan, and a crow, three of the five birds of alchemy. There are also symbols relating to Rosicrucianism. The first two houses have no less than six roses carved on them. Twice the Ten Commandments appear, with a sword laid across them. This may be a reference to the Knights Templar, as may a skull and crossbones on a tomb and a bearded head. When Wood was at Wetherby, he was living right within the centre of a ring of Templar properties. It is hard to believe that he would not have been intrigued by this mysterious sect. Hermes appears, perhaps representing Hermeticism. There are apparent symbols of Freemasonry, such as set squares and dividers. However, these are also related to alchemy.

One solution to the Circus suggested by Martin Wood, who has studied arcane and mainstream religions, is that it represents all beliefs. This is not impossible. One book of emblems refers to the rose garden of the philosophies and perhaps this is what Wood had in mind. If he was following in Toland's footsteps as a pantheist, this would make sense. Nevertheless, references to alchemy seem to outweigh all the rest. In particular there is the conjunction of the Circus and the Crescent. One of the themes of alchemy is the marriage of the sun and moon. The crescent clearly represents the moon but a circle alone is not representative of the sun in alchemy. It needs a dot in the centre. If the Circus was intended as the symbol of the sun, the reservoir of water, which took so much work to build, assumes a crucial significance. It completes the symbol. Can the King's Circus and the Royal Crescent, linked by Brock Street, possibly represent this alchemical wedding? Unlikely as it seems, one symbol suggests that it does. It is the Janus head on the southeast segment. There are Janus heads in several books, including Whitney's and Wither's, but there both heads are male. The two-headed being on the Circus appears to have one male and one female head – and seems to clinch it. Only in alchemy does that occur. The offspring of the sun and the moon is the hermaphroditic, two headed figure we have here in the Circus. In Basil Valentine's emblem book *Azoth*, this hermaphrodite stands on a circle, within which is a triangle and a square. Join the points where the roads enter the circus and you have your triangle. Below it is Queen Square. Suddenly Wood's dedication of surrounding villages to Roman gods and goddesses begins to fall into place, for all the ones he names have meanings for alchemists. And if you are tempted to dismiss this as too far-fetched to be true, remember Wood's hero "the great Sir Isaac Newton" – astronomer, mathematician, physicist – and alchemist.

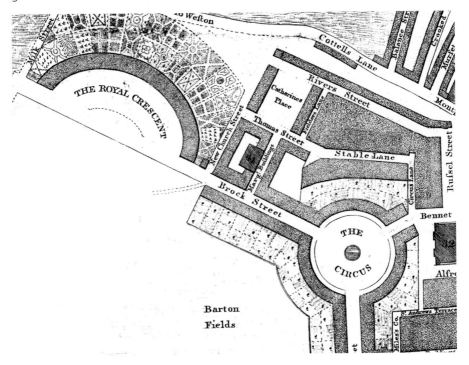

Looking at the carvings in the Circus can become compulsive. There is one which seems to represent Bath's Roman and Druid past, with fasces crossed with a wooden club. Did lease-holders have the right to select some emblems? There is evidence to show that they did. Pitt's house, and the one he leased later from Andrew Sproule after he had given up the earlier house, both have symbols of war and peace. Gainsborough, who adored music, has a carving representing music by his door. And one carving may have been chosen by Wood the Younger to represent the death of his father, for it shows an oak tree being blown down. It comes from Whitney's book, and the rhyme that goes with it is extremely apt, referring as it does to envy, hate, contempt and slander, echoing the obituary in the Bath Chronicle. Some, of course, were repaired and even recarved in the 1950s. but this happened to surprisingly few, perhaps no more than about ten, although what happened in earlier times we do not know. One is certainly modern. After restoration of the Circus in 1962, the stonemasons were allowed to carve a new metope with the tools of their trade. It bears the date.

Who knows what the truth about the Circus may be? Perhaps the Woods just saw it as a game. Perhaps in some architectural paradise they look down on us with amusement as we speculate and theorise. Whatever the truth, the Circus is a splendid finale to John Wood's works in Bath.

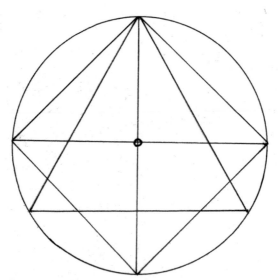

Geometric symbol which supports the two-headed offspring of the sun and the moon in Basil Valentine's *Azoth*.

8 EPILOGUE – ASSEMBLY ROOMS

The unknown factor in all of the speculation about John Wood is the role of his eldest son. "My chief assistant" is how he was described by his proud father. Doubtless his father was even prouder when his son went to Oxford University in March 1747, at the age of nineteen. He did not get his degree, but this was not uncommon in the eighteenth century. Intriguingly, his tutor was Joseph Wood – from Yorkshire. Was this a relation? Was there, after all, a connection between the Woods of Bath and the Woods of Yorkshire? University College was an unusual choice for a boy from the West Country, who would normally have chosen Exeter College. Joseph Wood was of quite humble birth, and worked his way through university as a servitor, before getting his degree. He was also the tutor to Doctor Johnson's friend Henry Thrale.

While at college, Wood the Younger probably studied many of the texts mentioned in his father's writings, such as Herodotus, Caesar, the letters of Pliny, and the works of Sallust, Tacitus and Suetonius. It shows how close their interests were. The two had worked together since the boy was thirteen years old, and perhaps longer, yet commentators have always differentiated beteen the two. Once it was fashionable to rate the son more highly than the father – now the pendulum seems to have swung the other way. Wood the Younger is considered to be pedestrian, uninspired. Looking at the Assembly Rooms we can see why. Would such a building in such a sensitive site get planning permission today? It seems unlikely. To be brutally frank – it's ugly. But the son was far more of a pragmatist than his father and he needed to be. Money difficulties were eventually to overwhelm him and he died in poverty. Here, at the Assembly Rooms, he was under pressure from the investors to be economical. They had, after all, turned down a scheme by no less an architect than Robert Adam because it was too expensive. The rooms did not need to be beautiful as long as they worked as Assembly Rooms – and they did. Inside the decoration was splendid and the facilities were all that could be desired. John Wood the Younger's maxim was "no architect can form a convenient plan unless he places himself in the situation of the person for whom he designs." If his father had followed that maxim he might not have ended up at loggerheads with Ralph Allen. Sadly, it is a maxim still ignored by some architects today. In fairness to John Wood the Younger, we should perhaps also consider his delightful rebuilding of the Hot Bath. It is not seen at its best these days, being swamped by Nicholas Grimshaw's glass and Bath Stone cube and sadly disfigured by Decimus Burton's totally unsuitable curtain wall, which, because it is Georgian, no one has had the courage to pull down. Devoid of these unhappy distractions, we would be able to see how well he managed to combine art and efficiency.

For all his pragmatism, it must be remembered that John Wood the Younger did not simply complete the Circus with its symbol-laden façade. He was responsible for its entire construction. It was he who built the Crescent – the temple to the Moon. It is bare of Druidical ornaments, as though he had put such things behind him. However, we know, from looking at the seal which Wood the Younger used, with its coat of arms derived from his father's, that he too proudly bore the oak tree as a personal symbol. He built into the leases of both the Circus and the Crescent a clause that stated if the builder did not complete the work on the façade precisely to the designs given, John Wood and his workmen could come in and put it right. Was this the action of a loyal son or a determined co-architect? We simply do not know what parts of the designs are his and what are his father's. We can only speculate.

Is there a point where one John Wood stopped and the other began, or are we looking at a master plan dreamt up by both of them? It's the final unanswered question.

PART THREE

UNANSWERED QUESTIONS

UNANSWERED QUESTIONS

This book set out to be a simple description of a walk around the city, explaining myths by and about John Wood. As time went on, the project grew and my researches led me into unfamiliar paths. I believe that there are many questions left to be answered – but I also believe that I am ill-equipped to find those answers. I do not have the necessary scholarship or resources to discover the truth. I hope that there are others out there who will take up the challenge. Here, then, are the questions which I think should be addressed.

1   How did John Wood know about Newton's investigations into Biblical chronology and Solomon's Temple?

2   Did John Wood meet William Stukeley?

3   Was there a connection between John Wood and the Italian architect Giacomo Leoni?

4   Was there a family connection between George Wither and John Wood through his wife, Jane Chivers? The presence of Wither's coat of arms in the wife's quarters of Wood's would suggest that there was.

5   Was John Wood's Coat of Arms ever registered with the College of Heralds, and if so, what was it – the version used on the book-plate or the version on his signet ring?

6   Where did John Wood have access to a collection of Emblem Books?

7   Did Lord Bingley, or any of his friends, have an interest in the arcane? Was it in his library that Wood found his inspiration?

8   Is there any evidence other than circumstantial to indicate that the owners of the houses in the Circus had any choice in the emblems?

9   What other evidence is there, apart from the building controls relating to the restoration in the 1950s, that the metopes have been altered?

10 What more is known about the connection between Andrew Sproule of Batheaston and John Wood the Younger? Sproule was the major shareholder in the Circus.

11 Is there a connection between John Wood of Bath and Joseph Wood of Yorkshire? The latter's home town was possibly Skelton – his writing is not clear.

12 Is there a point where one John Wood stopped and the other began, or are we looking at a master plan dreamt up by both of them?

WHAT DOES IT ALL MEAN?

The Ouroboros from the altarpiece by John Wood the Elder at Tyberton

BIBLIOGRAPHY

Books

Title	Publisher Name	Date	Ed	Author
The Holy Blood and the Holy Grail	Corgi Books	1984	6	Baigent, Leigh & Lincoln
The Unlocked Secret	William Kimber	1966	1	Dewar, James
Foucault's Pendulum	Random House	2001		Eco Umberto
Bath Pevsner Architectural Guide	Yale University Press	2003	1	Forsyth Michael
The Kingston Estate	Survey of Old Bath	1992	1	Holland,Elizabeth Chapman, Mike
John Wood Architect of Obsession	Millstream Books	1988	1	Mowl Tim & Earnshaw, Brian
Stonehenge, Neolithic Man and the Cosmos	Harper Collins	1996	1	North John
Abury, a Temple of the British Druids		1743	1	Stukeley William
Stonehenge, a Temple Restored to the British Druids		1740	1	Stukeley William
The Ten Books on Architecture	Dover	1960	2	Vitruvius (tr. M H Morgan)
The Last Sorcerer	Fourth Estate	1998	1	White Michael
Choir Gaure, vulgarly called Stonehenge		1747	1	Wood John
Description of Bath		1749	2	Wood John
Description of Bath		1765	3	Wood John
Description of Bath Vol 1		1742	1	Wood John
Description of Bath Vol 2		1743	1	Wood John
Description of Bath Vol 3		1743	1	Wood John
The Origin of Building		1741	1	Wood John

Documents

Document Title	Author	Date	Source	Location
Deeds of No 12 Royal Crescent				BRO
Building regulations, restoration work, The Circus		1950s		BRO
Deeds of The Circus, Queen Square and Gay Street		01/11/1754		BRO
Deeds of the Circus, Queen Square and Gay Street		04/11/1754		BRO
Deeds of Nos 4 The Circus				BRO
On Stanton Drew, Avebruy and Stonehenge	Bull, Larry		UWE	Internet
The Mystery of Bladud	Manco, Jean	July 1995	Bath City Life	Internet
Cursus-solving a 6,000 year old puzzle	McOmish, David	March 2003	British Archaeology	Internet
Isaac Newton Heretic	Snobelen, Steven D		Br l History Science	Internet
Stanton Drew	Voase, Nicola	Oct 2000	personal website	Internet
The Origin of Building (manuscript)	Wood, John			BRL
Essay on the External Use of Water	Smollett, Tobias	1752		

Websites on general subjects

Subject	Address
Alchemy	www.levity.com/alchemy
Emblematic Books	http://emblem.libraries.psu.edu/overview.htm
Rosicrucian Texts	http://www.crcsite.org/library.htm

INDEX

IN MEMORIAM

JOHN WOOD
1704 – 1754

The mighty oak, that shrinks not with a blast,
But stiffly stands, when Boreas most doth blow
With rage thereof, is broken down at last,
When bending reeds, that couch in tempests low,
With yielding still, do safe and sound appear:
And look aloft, when that the clouds be clear.

When Envy, Hate, Contempt, and Slander rage:
Which are the storms and tempests of this life,
With patience then, we must the combat wage,
And not with force resist their deadliest strife.
But suffer still, and then we shall in fine,
Our foes subdue, when they with shame shall pine.

From *A Choice of Emblems*
Geoffrey Whitney